Everyday Asian

$\mathcal{E}$*veryday*
Asian

From Soups to Noodles, From Barbecues

to Curries, Your Favorite Asian Recipes

Made Easy

Marnie Henricksson

HarperCollins books may be purchased for educational, business, or sales promotional use. For information please write: Special Markets Department, HarperCollins Publishers Inc., 10 East 53rd Street, New York, NY 10022.

FIRST EDITION

Designed by Nicola Ferguson

Printed on acid-free paper

Library of Congress Cataloging-in-Publication Data

Henricksson, Marnie.
Everyday Asian / Marnie Henricksson.—1st ed.
p.   cm.
Includes index.
ISBN 0-06-008466-9
1. Cookery, Asian.   I. Title.
TX724.5.A1 H45   2003
641.595—dc21   2002032731

03 04 05 06 07 WBC/QW 10 9 8 7 6 5 4 3 2 1

for Russell

Contents

Acknowledgments

i am lucky to have lots of support from my family in all things, including cooking. My two sisters helped me tremendously with this project. Lisa Henricksson, who has given me cookbooks and food magazines routinely over the years, helped edit the manuscript and came up with the title. She has also been a willing recipe tester. Ann Henricksson worked with me at the restaurant, helped me with wine pairings in the book, and has turned out to be a tireless recipe tester. Thank you both. I would also like to thank my parents, John and Julie Henricksson, for (among other things) having "Japanese night" in our suburban Minnesota home during my childhood, when we would move the coffee table into the middle of the livingroom and cook sukiyaki on it—my introduction to Asian food. Their support and love has never waned for a moment.

I would like to thank Markus Alkire for his never failing good spirits and for keeping me up-to-date on the New York restaurant scene. Also, thank you to Gerri Hirshey, a friend who has served as a model to me, showing that one can have a successful career and still take the time to be a wonderful home cook and host. Thanks also to Brian Tobin, who gave me an introduction to the real Japan, taking me to countless Tokyo restaurants, and who believed in me to the point of investing in the restaurant. Thanks also to Harry Bromer, my other silent partner.

I would also like to thank everyone who worked at my restaurant, especially Akim, Justo, Rosa, Mimi, Douglas, Deborah, Liz, Tara, Randi, Brian, my sister Ann, and my husband Russell. We had a good run thanks to you.

To my editor Harriet Bell, thank you for being gentle with a first-time author. And to my agent and friend Anne Edelstein, for believing she could sell this book.

My biggest thank you goes to my husband, Russell, who has seen, felt, and tasted life with me for the last twenty-two years. This book has most definitely been a group effort for us. Even during a very busy year for him, he helped with writing, editing, and the pesky computer, not to mention tasting the food every night—and there was no complaining.

Everyday Asian

Introduction

i believe Asian food remains a mystery to most American cooks. They love the complex flavors of Thai and Chinese, the clean simplicity of Japanese, the herb-infused freshness of Vietnamese, but for the most part they avoid these cuisines in their own kitchens. That is one reason that so many people came to my restaurant and enjoyed the food during the six years I owned and operated a successful Asian noodle shop in New York City.

Once I had had two children and moved out of the city, I realized that cooking Asian at home requires thought. While there are many Asian cookbooks, most are impractical for the average home cook. They require too many unfamiliar or hard-to-get ingredients; special cooking equipment and techniques can be daunting or are simply impractical in a home kitchen. I came to the conclusion that these cookbooks merely whet people's appetites for Asian food and send them to restaurants like mine. Could I come up with some practical, everyday techniques and recipes that might help the home cook create the kind of food I had fallen in love with?

My Asian cooking journey began when my husband and I spent a year in Tokyo in the mid 1980s. Living in a neighborhood on the outskirts of the city, where Westerners were rare (the dry cleaner didn't bother with my name but simply labeled my clothes *gaijin,* or "foreigner"), I cooked using the ingredients available at the local grocery store. All I had in our Japanese-style apartment was a two-burner hot plate, a half fridge, and a sink, but I could buy Japanese eggplant, more varieties and cuts of fish than I had ever seen, fresh soybeans, fresh tofu made daily by a shop that sold nothing else, a zillion varieties of miso, shiso leaves, the cellophane-packed makings for sukiyaki, and on and on. So I cooked. I prepared Western-style fried chicken using Japanese panko breading. I simmered spaghetti sauce with enoki mushrooms. I made my own versions of Japanese food and soon realized that a good cook uses what is available. We also ate out frequently at little hole-in-the-wall family-run restaurants. These were humble places often with nothing more than a few stools for customers, but they served simple, delicious food.

After we left Japan, we embarked on a long, slow trip through Southeast Asia—a trip that changed my life. I sat on beaches in Thailand downing searing bowls of *tom yum* soup. In ethereal restaurants set amid the rice terraces of Bali, I ate smoked duck, shrimp sambal, and satay. I absorbed the unique blend of Singapore's cuisines—Indian, Chinese, and the Malaysian hybrid called Nonya—at neon-lit hawker stands. The wafting odor of fried garlic that perfumes the air of Seoul went right to my head. That was it—I was hooked. The foods of Asia are infinitely varied and exotic, but earthy. They use locally produced ingredients to the very best advantage. Asians tend to eat small amounts of highly seasoned food accompanied by rice and noodles. The food made sense to me and it made me happy. I knew that *this* was what I wanted to do.

In 1991 I opened Marnie's Noodle Shop in New York City—a tiny restaurant with a counter and a few tables that brought to mind the many mom-and-pop establishments I had visited in Japan. In my restaurant, I put to use what I had learned in my travels. Despite its tiny size, it was an immediate hit, and I like to think that was because my love for the food and spices of Asia came through in every dish.

So this cookbook is born of my experience—first as an impressionable traveler, then as the owner of an Asian restaurant, and later as a home cook who had to find ways to make my recipes work in a standard kitchen. My style is hearty and flavorful, more peasant than refined. I had droves of regular customers, some of whom came three, four, or five times a week—the best testament to a cook's sensibility. My clients in Greenwich Village included a wide spectrum of people, from celebrities and families to laborers and Wall Street types. Many of the dishes I served developed over time: since my noodle shop was a tiny space, I spent a lot of time chatting with my customers, experimenting and learning how to please people. The hallmarks of my style are less oil and sugar than might be found in traditional recipes, more vegetables, freshly ground spices, and fresh and flavorful local ingredients, even if they aren't exactly what would be used in Asia.

I have always cherished a few of my cookbooks—not because they were comprehensive or beautiful travelogues, or written by famous people, but because I could count on them. The recipes work; the results never vary. I hope these recipes will accomplish just that and give the home cook a steady hand with everyday Asian food as well as some great recipes for casual entertaining.

Every aspiring Asian cook should have recipes for a great pad Thai, tried-and-true Chinese roast pork, well-made sesame noodles, simple spring rolls, and a delicious version of the meaty Vietnamese soup called pho. *Everyday Asian* gives you those recipes. The recipes are relatively easy and allow most of the work to be done in advance. Of course, they use Asian ingredients, but nothing is hard to find or esoteric. If you see an unfamiliar ingredient in a recipe, look it up in the ingredients chapter (where it's appropriate there, I even offer the brand name of the product I use). And if you live in an area that has no Asian markets, mail-order sources are given at the end of the book.

I have strong feelings about Asian food: it is where my heart is. I like it simple and fresh, with lots of herbs and chiles. I like lightening dishes with lemon and lime juice. I like caramelizing onions and sautéing greens. I like to douse a profusion of vegetables in spicy coconut curry. I like fried morsels with salty, sweet, sour, and spicy dipping sauces. Maybe most of all, I love rice and noodles—the honest, endlessly variable staples of Asian cuisine. I relish the opportunity to share my version of everyday Asian food.

Ingredients

As a restaurant cook, I was spoiled. Exotic ingredients were just a phone call away. Fresh noodles and bean sprouts were delivered from Chinatown. If a special cut of meat was required, I called the butcher and added it to my order. My greengrocer supplied me with tofu and fresh lemongrass. On my biweekly trips to a Vietnamese market in Chinatown, I was able to buy fresh Thai basil and Chinese sausages at very reasonable prices.

Now that I have to rely on my none-too-adventurous suburban supermarket, I appreciate how hard it is to obtain Asian ingredients. Depending on where you live and how rigorously authentic you want to be, if you want to explore Asian cuisine you have to be either intrepid—searching high and low for ingredients—or enterprising. Fortunately, as supermarkets around the country have expanded their international food and produce sections in recent years, many essentials such as rice vinegar, chiles, and dried Asian noodles are now easier to find. However, some of the things necessary for these recipes can be purchased only from an Asian grocer or by mail order. Many of them have long shelf lives, so once you've schlepped to a Chinatown or ordered through the mail, you won't have to do it again soon. I now only shop in New York City's Chinatown bimonthly. A source guide at the end of the book gives several good Asian mail-order websites.

Chicken Stock

I keep a supply of chicken stock in the refrigerator and use it frequently to add a bit of richness to sauces. Many recipes in this book call for poached chicken; save the poaching liquid, which yields a nice, all-purpose chicken broth. Keep wing tips, backbones, and other bits from cut-up chickens in the freezer so stock makings are on hand.

Liquid chicken stock that is canned (Swanson or College Inn) or comes in cardboard containers (Kitchen Basics or Swanson) is the second-best alternative. The recipes in this book call for a stock with little or no salt, so taste and adjust accordingly. You can also use Knorr cubes. An Asian variety of Knorr chicken stock with some extra fat is pretty good. Avoid Wyler, as it has an intrusive taste.

The best, least expensive stock is your own poaching liquid. By adding ginger slices, peppercorns, and scallions to the broth, it will become complex.

Chiles

For fresh chiles, use jalapeños and serranos, which are available year-round in supermarkets. The medium-hot jalapeño is plump, green, and two to three inches long. Serranos are green, much thinner, and about the same length. Serranos are usually hotter than jalapeños, but taste a chile before using it, because the strength varies tremendously. Hot Thai "bird" or "bird's eye" chiles are tiny and usually sold when green. In general, the smaller the chile, the hotter it is.

Dried chiles have a more consistent heat level and obviously keep longer. I generally use them for cooked dishes and the fresh green chiles for cold dishes. All dried chiles are red because they are dried once they ripen. You can get bags of dried two- to three-inch-long chiles in some supermarkets, Latin or Asian markets, spice shops, Indian shops, and some greengrocers.

When cooking with chiles, wash your hands well after cutting or breaking them up. Do not wipe your eyes when preparing them. I am not a fan of removing seeds from chiles to tone them down. If you want less heat, use less chile.

Chili Oil

Chili oil is simply soybean or vegetable oil that has been infused with dried red chiles. The color is red or orange, and it is very hot. A few drops are all that is necessary to give heat to a dish. Some bottled brands have additives like anise to keep them from spoiling. Any brand will do.

You can make your own chili oil by adding 1 tablespoon crushed dried red chiles to 1 cup canola oil in a small saucepan. Heat the oil over medium heat for 5 minutes, but do not boil. Remove from the heat and let it rest for an hour. Strain through a sieve and put in a tightly lidded jar.

Chili Sauce and Sambal Olek

There are a daunting number of chili sauces and derivative chile products on the Asian grocer's shelf, but to keep it simple, I suggest just two for these recipes. The first is the smooth sriracha chili sauce. The most readily available brand is called Tuong Ot Sriracha, which is produced in California and has a rooster on the label. Often used as a table condiment in Thai and Vietnamese restaurants, it contains chiles, vinegar, garlic, and sugar.

I also use Southeast Asian sambal olek, which is a chunky chili sauce with similar ingredients but no sugar. The brand I use, called Sambal Oelek, is made by the same company as the sriracha, Huy Fong Foods, with the rooster on the label. You may substitute other chili sauces, but read the ingredients to make sure they don't contain additives.

Chinese Sausage

These hard, six-inch sausages, known as lop chong, are made from pork, pork fat, wine, and sugar. They are sold in 1-pound packages or by the piece in Asian markets. Since they're hard, like salami, they need to be either steamed or sautéed before going into a stir-fry. They have a sweet, porky flavor, and there is really no substitute for them. When you find them, buy a lot; they will keep for weeks in the refrigerator or months in the freezer.

Citrus

In Southeast Asia, citrus leaves and rind are used in addition to the juice to perfume a dish. Asian limes tend to be smaller and more fragrant. I use only fresh lemon and lime juice or zest. When shopping for lemons and limes, look for slightly soft ones with thin skins; they will be the juiciest.

Coconut Milk

Coconut milk—not to be confused with the watery stuff inside a fresh coconut—adds a distinctive creaminess to Asian food. To make your own coconut milk from fresh coconuts, as they do all over Southeast Asia, grate fresh coconut meat (or pulse it in a food processor), cover it with hot water for a few minutes, and then strain the liquid through a fine sieve, pressing the remaining mush with the back of a spoon.

Unsweetened coconut milk, a convenient substitute, is available in 14-ounce cans. It doesn't have to be an Asian brand—there are acceptable West Indian brands available—but make sure it contains only coconut milk, water, and a preservative. Look for Thai brands such as Chaokoh, in the brown and white can, or Chef's Choice, in the blue can. Always stir well before using. Once opened, the milk will keep for about a week in the refrigerator.

Crispy Fried Onions, Shallots, and Garlic

Crispy fried bits are used as garnishes and to add savory crunchiness to salads, stir-fried dishes, and noodles. I make a big batch and keep it in the refrigerator in a tightly lidded jar for a month. Slice one large onion, the equivalent in shallots, or 2 garlic bulbs as thinly as possible. (Onions that are sliced too thick will become soggy and unusable after they've been fried.) Heat 1 to 2 cups of canola oil over medium heat in a small skillet. When it's hot, add the onions. Stir to separate the pieces and let them gently fry until crisp and deep brown, but not burned. Keep a close eye on them because they can go from perfectly fried to black in seconds. Onions take about twenty minutes, but shallots and garlic will take only ten to fifteen minutes. When they're done, remove with a slotted spoon and drain on a paper towel. Once they're cool, either use them immediately or put them in an airtight jar. Use the flavored cooking oil for salad dressings or sautéing. A refrigerated jar of this oniony oil will keep for months. There's no need to strain the oil; a few flecks of onion in the oil only adds to the flavor.

Curry Paste

Thai curry paste is a spicy flavor base made with chiles, lemongrass, galangal, cilantro root, shrimp paste, spices, garlic, shallots, and salt. The paste is usually fried in a little oil or coconut milk, which provides the base for a sauce. At my restaurant, I made my own but wasn't always satisfied with my version. Fresh galangal is hard to find, the frozen variety contains too much water, and dried galangal never softens enough when hydrated. Fresh lemongrass, which I can't always find in my local supermarket, is also essential to the paste, so I now use a canned variety by Maesri. They make green, red, yellow and other curry pastes; each is a variation with different spicing and fresh or dried chiles.

Only canned red curry paste is used in these recipes. Because dried chiles are used in the paste, the taste of the canned version most closely matches the real thing. Check to see that the brand you buy does not contain MSG or other additives. A 4-ounce can costs less than a dollar and only a tablespoon or two is used at a time. Curry paste, once opened, lasts for about a month in the refrigerator if it is tightly covered.

Dashi

Dashi, the all-purpose Japanese stock used in soups, marinades, sauces, and dressings, is made from kombu (a dried seaweed) and dried bonito fish shavings. Simmer a 4-inch piece of kombu in 4 cups of water for 10 minutes. Add 1 cup of bonito flakes, cover, and remove from the heat. Let the mixture sit for 5 minutes, then strain. "Dashi-no-moto" is the instant version, which I use a great deal. They're packaged like tea bags; just pop one into 4 cups water, let it simmer for 5 to 10 minutes, then remove the bag. I prefer the Maruhachi Muramatsu product, but any brand without MSG is fine. Bonito flakes, kombu, and dashi-no-moto are available in areas with a large Japanese population in grocery stores or by mail order.

Fish Sauce

Fish sauce is made from salted, fermented anchovies or shrimp. Use fish sauce for seasoning as you would soy sauce or salt. There are many styles in Asian markets, ranging from thin, light caramel-colored sauces to opaque ones with pieces of anchovy floating in them. Generally, the darker the color, the more intense the flavor. Fish sauce is manufactured mainly in Thailand (where it is called nam pla), Vietnam (nuoc mam), and the Philippines (patis). The Thai brands, commonly available in this country, are less intense than the Vietnamese and fine for all-purpose cooking. In my restaurant I used the Thai brands Squid, Tiparos, and Healthy Boy, and was satisfied with all of them. Asian chefs often use finer quality fish sauces for dipping sauces and lesser ones for cooking. A home cook, however, is unlikely to have more than one bottle in the kitchen, and it takes forever to use it up. Fortunately, it lasts indefinitely on the shelf, although I refrigerate it.

Five-Spice Powder

This intense Chinese spice mixture is easy to make at home. The number five is more symbolic of healthfulness than accurate, since different variations call for anywhere from five to seven spices. The predominant aroma is licorice because of the fennel and star anise. It is best to grind your own spices and to do so in small amounts so the spices retain their strength. Combine 1 teaspoon fennel seeds, 1 teaspoon whole cloves, 2 whole star anise, a 2-inch cinnamon stick, and 1 tablespoon Szechuan peppercorns in a clean coffee grinder. Grind thoroughly until you have a powder. If you want to buy it ready-made, five-spice powder can be found in the international section of most supermarkets. As with all spices, keep it tightly covered and away from the light.

Garam Masala

This dark Indian spice mixture lends food a dusky sharpness either as a condiment or when added at the end of the cooking process. Its flavor is quite different from that of curry powder, so do not use it as a substitute. There are many recipes for garam masala, and this one calls for black cardamom seeds as the dominant flavor, a spice that "warms" the body. Combine the following ingredients in a clean coffee grinder: 1 tablespoon black cardamom seeds, 1 teaspoon black peppercorns, a 2-inch cinnamon stick, 1 teaspoon cumin seeds (black cumin if you have it), 1 teaspoon whole cloves, a quarter of a nutmeg. Grind to a powder. It is best if used within a week but can be stored in a tightly lidded jar for a month or two. You can buy garam masala pre-ground at Indian and spice shops.

Ginger and Galangal

The tang of fresh ginger is absolutely essential to Asian cooking. It is even considered to be health-giving and is used as a tonic for almost any ailment. Fortunately, ginger root is widely available in most markets. Look for a chunk that is not dried out and shriveled looking. When you break off a piece, the inside should have a greenish tint and be extremely fragrant. It should not have a woody texture. Unless otherwise stated in the recipe, ginger is always peeled. Never use powdered ginger as a substitute.

Galangal is a rhizome of a different color, both literally and figuratively. Also sometimes referred to by its Indonesian name, *laos*, it looks somewhat like ginger but is yellowish with dark rings around it and has a medicinal taste and a woody texture. Fresh galangal is extremely hard to come by. You can find it dried in Asian stores, but in this form it's useful only in soups and braised dishes. I have had no luck soaking it and then grinding it for spice pastes. I have tried it frozen, but it disintegrates when thawed. Consequently, I don't use galangal much in this book, but I do suggest when to use it if you can obtain it.

Herbs

Southeast Asians love to use fresh herbs in their food. Herbs are thrown in during the last few minutes of cooking, used to garnish a bowl of soup, tossed in a salad, or rolled up with a bit of meat or seafood in a lettuce leaf or rice paper. However you use them, they add another dimension to any dish.

Many Asian herbs are not grown here or are only marginally available, but don't let that stop you from using the herbs that we do have. The big three that go well with these recipes are cilantro, mint, and basil.

Cilantro, also known as coriander or Chinese parsley, is the most popular Asian herb, and every bit of it is used in cooking: leaves, stems, roots, and seeds. (Parsley should not be used as a substitute.) Thai cooks use the roots, which have a peppery, green flavor, in marinades and spice pastes. Cilantro attracts dirt, so soak it in a bowl of water before spinning it dry. The soft green stems can be used along with the leaves, but remove the lower stems or any dark, hard stems.

Mint is so refreshing and accessible that my daughter eats it straight from our garden. Several Vietnamese varieties are not available here, but spearmint or garden mint are appropriate for our purposes and easily found in grocery stores. The stems are hard and tough, so just use the leaves.

Thai basil, or Asian basil, is available in many markets now, and if you can find it, use it. It has a purplish stem, small green leaves, and often flowers. It has a stronger anise flavor than Italian basil and arrives at the market very clean, so you need only to lightly rinse it. If Thai basil is not available, by all means use Italian basil rather than omit it altogether. The Italian basil will brighten the dish. Basil is now available year-round and is another easy herb to grow. I haven't had much success growing Asian basil, but Italian basil does very well in the garden and keeps coming back all summer. Use only the leaves and flowers, and since the leaves of Italian basil can be quite large, tear them into smaller pieces in these recipes.

Hoisin Sauce

A sweet, smooth soybean sauce often served as a table condiment in Asian restaurants. I find the flavor overpowering when used in this way but very nice when used sparingly in a marinade or stew for meat or tofu. I prefer Koon Chun brand in the 15-ounce jar, but there are many other brands in the international food section of grocery stores.

Kaffir Lime Leaf

Used whole in soups or julienned in curries or salads, the flat, shiny, double leaves of the Kaffir lime tree add distinctive citrusy notes. Kaffir lime is a defining ingredient in Thai cooking but, sadly, it is difficult to find fresh here. To prepare it, remove the leaves from the stem and if julienning it, remove the central vein. If you can't find it fresh, kaffir lime leaves are available in dried and frozen forms, which are best just used in soups or curries. All three varieties are available from mail-order sources in this book, though the fresh leaves are quite expensive. It is possible to grow your own kaffir lime in a pot, which will provide a small supply of leaves. To give a dish a similar lift, use lemon or lime zest. The effect is not the same, but it's better than omitting it altogether.

Krupah

These dried shrimp crackers, made of egg white and shrimp, come uncooked and look like hard little disks. When dropped in hot oil, they puff up to three times their size. They have a pleasant shrimpy taste and are nice and crunchy. You can serve them as an appetizer or put a few on the plate of most any Southeast Asian meal. They cook in a matter of seconds, so don't be put off cooking them. Just turn on your deep-fryer or heat a few cups of canola oil in a small skillet over medium heat and drop one in for a test. If the oil is hot enough, it should puff up immediately. Turn briefly, then remove with a slotted spoon and drain on paper towels. They are sometimes available already puffed, but the bags are easily crushed and they taste much better if freshly fried. Both varieties are available from Asian grocers or by mail order under many brand names.

Lemongrass

Lemongrass is a tall, rough, light gray-green grass native to Southeast Asia. Its citrus aroma and flavor make it a key ingredient in Southeast Asian cuisines. Fresh lemongrass is always preferable. Depending on where you live, your grocery store may carry it. Cut off the bottom where the root starts and peel off the outside layer. Use only the white part and either slice it into very thin rounds or shred it in a coffee grinder, or cut it into two-inch pieces and bruise it with the side of a knife (for soups). You can also freeze it for up to three months. If its not available fresh, there is a dried variety, available in 1-ounce packages in Asian stores or by mail order. It has a pleasant aroma, and I have used it in soups, but it doesn't taste much like the real thing. Roland brand sells it preserved in 7-ounce jars, which I have used successfully in marinades, stir-fries, and soups. I have grown lemongrass in a pot, but after a full season, I had enough only for soup.

Miso

Miso is a paste made from fermented soybeans, another grain such as rice or barley, and salt. It has a distinctive savory, salty taste. It is an aged product and lasts for six months in the refrigerator. It is used in soups, as a marinade, and in dressings, and is spread on all manner of fish, vegetables, and tofu to be grilled. There are many varieties ranging in color from creamy white to various shades of yellow to red to deep brown. For my purposes, I use yellow (shinshu miso) and red (aka miso). The shinshu is inexpensive, salty, and all-purpose, and the aka is more complex and good for spreading on items to be grilled. In general, the lighter in color the miso, the sweeter the taste. The darker the paste, the saltier and the more intense the flavor, as it has been aged longer. Miso, so rich in protein, is available from Japanese grocers, health food stores, and sometimes supermarkets.

Mushrooms

Dried black mushrooms, labeled variously as Chinese, black, or shiitake mushrooms, add robust flavor and meatiness to many Asian dishes. Look for mushrooms with thick caps with deep white grooves. You may find only one kind in your supermarket, but when you get to an Asian store, try one of the more expensive varieties and note the difference. The mushrooms need to be soaked in warm water until soft, for about thirty minutes. Remove the stems before using. The Japanese soak these mushrooms in cool water for up to twenty-four hours, which they claim better preserves the flavor and allows the entire mushroom to be eaten, stem and all. I always save the mushroom soaking liquid to add to the dish later. Just make sure you strain off the gritty bits that have settled at the bottom of the bowl.

I use dried black mushrooms, canned straw mushrooms, and fresh shiitake and portobello mushrooms. If you can't get dried mushrooms, use fresh shiitakes instead, readily available in grocery stores. If you can't get either, use portobellos before resorting to white button mushrooms. Canned straw mushrooms are always stocked in the international food sections of most large grocery stores.

Noodles

CELLOPHANE NOODLES These noodles are made from mung bean starch and are sold in little white bundles. Lungkow Vermicelli seems to be the most ubiquitous brand. Once they are soaked and cooked, they become transparent and gelatinous. They have little flavor of their own but are excellent for soaking up sauces. The bundles are sometimes tied with string, so be sure to remove the string before using. They should be soaked in water for fifteen minutes or until soft before being added to soups or stir-fries or boiled for a few minutes to be used cold. I find it best to cut them into six-inch lengths with scissors after soaking or boiling. They come in different-sized packages, but I buy the 3.5-ounce.

CHINESE EGG NOODLES At the restaurant I used only fresh egg noodles, but now that I can't get them so easily, I have found that I actually prefer the dried ones because they stand up better to cooking. While there are many brands, I suggest buying the thin rather than the flat ones; the thin ones are perfect for cold noodle dishes and soups. Cook the noodles in boiling, unsalted water for five to eight minutes. They are usually packaged in little bundles, so loosen the bundles with tongs as they cook. When you taste a strand to see if it is done, it should remain a little chewy. To keep the noodles from clumping in cold dishes, I toss them with a half cup of warm chicken broth after they drain. In many cases, you can substitute #9 spaghetti or angel hair pasta.

RICE PAPER WRAPPERS Used to make spring rolls or wrap up bits of grilled food, rice papers are made from cooked rice and water and therefore don't need to be cooked, just moistened. Circular rice papers come in transparent boxes in six-, eight-, and twelve-inch sizes. I use the smaller size of any Vietnamese brand I find. Each package contains a whole lot, so you can get three or four dishes out of a single package, even if several sheets are torn. There are many ways to treat them, but what works best for me is to have a bowl of medium hot water on the prep table and dip the paper in for a second. I lay the paper on the work surface and commence filling it. By the time I start rolling, they are the perfect consistency. They can be eaten raw or deep-fried once filled.

RICE NOODLES Also called rice sticks or rice vermicelli, these come in various widths and shapes. They are made of rice flour and water. I use the medium width, dried, flat rice noodles called *banh pho* for the rice noodle dishes in this book. I like the Erawan brand, an easily found Thai variety with a green label that comes in 1-pound bags. Rice noodles must be soaked in water for thirty minutes and drained before cooking. In stir-fried dishes, the texture is best if you do not cook the noodles before adding them to the dish. For soups, cook the noodles in boiling water for a minute or two, drain them, and then pour hot broth over them. I also use them in cold salads, after boiling them in advance.

SOBA This is my favorite Japanese noodle. Supposedly, the more buckwheat (which is not a member of the wheat family) and less wheat flour the noodle contains, the higher the quality. Those noodles, however, are very expensive and not as pleasantly chewy as those with some wheat flour.

A great deal of lore surrounds the cult of soba. To learn how to make and hand cut great soba requires years of training, much like the schooling of a sushi chef. The dried soba available in supermarkets and Asian groceries are just fine. Cook the soba in boiling water for eight to ten minutes. Taste a noodle to see if its done; it should be slightly chewy. Soba noodles are earthy in flavor and can be used in many ways, such as in a simple traditional broth, served cold with a dipping sauce, or in a salad with a simple soy vinaigrette.

WHEAT NOODLES I like to use the linguine-shaped Chinese Canton noodle, the square Chinese Shanghai noodle, or the flat Japanese udon for any recipe with a sauce that needs to be soaked up. They are expecially good with coconut milk sauces. I draw the line when it comes to substituting an Italian pasta like linguine when coconut milk is used, as it won't soak up the sauce properly. Cook the noodles in boiling, unsalted water for eight to ten minutes until just done, then add to the sauce, where they'll cook a bit more. I now see fresh, thin wheat noodles available in the organic produce section of grocery stores (where you also find tofu). Use these if you cannot get one of the other wheat noodles I mention.

Oil

Peanut oil is used most often in Asia for cooking because it is available, has a high smoking point so it doesn't burn quickly, and imparts a good flavor. If you have it, use it. Although peanut was the oil of choice at my restaurant, I find at home that I don't cook at very high temperatures, so I have taken to using canola oil. It is a healthy oil, inexpensive, and doesn't interfere with the flavor of the dish. Do not use olive oil.

Onions, Shallots, Garlic, and Scallions

In Southeast Asia, shallots are the onion of choice. In these recipes I generally use yellow onions for cooking because shallots can be expensive here, especially in the quantities needed. Use shallots if you have them, using your judgment to figure out an equivalent amount. I use red onions in place of shallots when they are to be eaten raw, but use shallots if you have them.

Garlic cloves vary tremendously in size. In my recipes, I always use a clove as a unit of measure. By a clove I mean a medium-sized clove, unless I specify otherwise. Buy garlic that is in tight, white bulbs.

Scallions (also called spring onions or green onions) are essential to Chinese, Korean, and Japanese cooking. They don't last as long as these other onions, so buy them a bunch at a time. To clean them, cut off the end with the root and peel the first layer of skin off. My Chinese chef always slit the white part lengthwise and then chopped them.

Peanuts

For all the recipes in this book, start with raw hulled peanuts. Roast them in a 350°F-degree oven or toaster oven for fifteen minutes until golden brown, cool them, and then chop them up. You can get them from an Asian grocer or from a health food store. Don't use dry roasted peanuts as a substitute.

Rice

I use jasmine rice and Japanese short-grain rice for most all Asian meals. Jasmine rice is a long-grain rice with a unique fragrance. I buy a 10- or 20-pound bag when shopping at an Asian grocer's, since I use so much of it. There are many grades of rice, and the more expensive, the better. I buy the "extra fancy" variety of whatever brand I can find. Use Thai rice, if possible, but as an alternative, I find the American-grown Jasmati a good choice. I also serve Indian basmati rice with Asian meals. The grains are even more separate than those of jasmine rice and it has a nutty aroma. The American grown basmati rice called Texmati is also acceptable.

Short-grain rice is a little sticky and somewhat shiny when cooked. It's really the appropriate choice for a Japanese or Korean meal. It is available in many stores now, sometimes even in supermarkets. I see Kokuho Rose or Nishiki brand most often and both are good. Jasmine and short-grain rice are very different and yet I crave both. Sometimes I cook Japanese short-grain rice with a Thai meal and it works out beautifully, so don't be afraid to experiment with what you like best.

To cook rice, put rice in a saucepan or rice cooker (I usually make 2 cups dry rice for four people) and then add water to one knuckle width above the rice. If using a saucepan, bring the rice to a boil, cover, and reduce heat to very low. The rice will be done in twenty minutes. Do not lift the lid. In a rice cooker, just close it up and turn it on. I do not soak or rinse rice; I don't find it necessary with the rice we buy.

Rice Wine and Mirin

Chinese or Shaoxing rice wine is a staple in Chinese cooking. It is amber colored and usually comes in 750-ml bottles. My preferred brand comes in a rectangular bottle with a red label in Chinese and a small white label at the bottom that says "Shaoshing." Dry sherry is a reasonable substitute.

Mirin is the syrupy sweet Japanese rice wine used in soups, dressings, and marinades. Look for "hon-mirin" on the bottle, which means it is naturally brewed, not "aji-mirin," which is just a mass of sweeteners and salt. Kikkoman makes both varieties.

Salted Black Beans

Salted, fermented soybeans are one of life's great culinary bargains. You use them by the tablespoon and a big, 17-ounce can-shaped cardboard box costs sixty-five cents—or it did four years ago when I bought the box I am currently working on. I don't think they ever go bad in the refrigerator. I use Yang Jiang Preserved Beans. They also come in plastic bags and jars. They add a nice savory flavor to fish, tofu, and chicken.

Sesame Oil

Sesame oil is an amber-colored oil extracted from toasted sesame seeds. Intensely flavored and used in small amounts, it is one of the most frequently used ingredients in this book. Look for pure sesame oil, not a blend. I prefer Kadoya brand, a Japanese sesame oil. "Toasted sesame oil" and "sesame oil" are the same thing. Grocery stores now routinely carry sesame oil in the international food section.

Sesame Paste

Sesame paste, made from toasted ground sesame seeds, is used for making sauces and dressings. I prefer Lan Chi brand, which is labeled "Sesame Seed Paste" or "Chinese Salad Dressing" and comes in 8-ounce jars. The oil separates and comes to the top, so try to incorporate it back in as you measure. Middle Eastern tahini is an acceptable substitute although lighter in color, since it is made from hulled raw seeds and it doesn't have the nutty flavor.

Shrimp Sauces, Powders, and Pastes

DRIED SHRIMP AND DRIED SHRIMP POWDER Tiny dried shrimp are used as a salty seasoning all over Asia. I like them to flavor soup broths and salad dressings and toss into Thai salads. I even like to munch on them for a snack. (The powdered form is good for salad dressings and as a substitute for whole dried shrimp.) Whole shrimp should be pinkish orange, not brown, and the larger, the better. They are frequently soaked in water to soften, but this is not strictly necessary. There are many qualities available in Asian markets, generally sold in 8-ounce plastic packages. The best dried shrimp are stored in wooden barrels and sold by the ounce. They all need to be refrigerated. Many other dried sea products, such as oysters, squid, scallops, shark's fin, and mussels are also used as seasonings.

SHRIMP SAUCE AND DRIED SHRIMP PASTE Shrimp sauce and paste are probably the most pungent flavorings found in Southeast Asian cooking. Cooks in this country use them sparingly, but don't let the odor scare you off; they mellow when cooked and add a very important flavor to the dish. I use the Koon Chun brand of shrimp sauce which is widely available. Dried shrimp paste is generally sold here by its Malaysian name, *blachan*, or sometimes *belacan*. Also known as *trasi* in Indonesia and *kapi* in Thailand, it comes in 8-ounce bricks. One brick lasts quite a while when well wrapped in paper inside a zippered plastic bag in the refrigerator.

Szechuan Peppercorns

Sometimes labeled "anise pepper," these reddish-brown berries are not a member of the pepper family at all. The pods are from the prickly ash tree. American Indians used the bark of this tree to numb the mouth in the case of a toothache. It is their hulls that impart the most flavor, not their seeds. The peppercorns have a marvelous aroma when toasted and add that same, mouth-numbing aspect to roasted meats and chicken. You can make a simple seasoning salt with them that's great to have in your repertoire. (See the recipe for Roast Chicken with Szechuan Peppercorns on page 144.) Once they are roasted and ground, use them right away, as the flavor dissipates quickly. They're sold in spice shops, Asian grocers, and by mail order.

Soy Sauce

Soy sauce is the distinctive salty flavoring of many Asian countries. Made from salted, fermented soybeans in liquid form, soy sauce comes in many degrees of saltiness, shades of brown, and consistencies. In this book, when I refer to soy sauce I mean light soy, and mushroom soy for dark soy. Unfortunately, there is little variety available in grocery stores. The light Japanese Kikkoman brand is universally available (I do not mean Kikkoman "lite" soy sauce), although Yamasa brand seems to be favored by the Japanese. If you can get to an Asian market, Pearl River Brand Superior Soy is a good Chinese light soy sauce. For a dark sauce, I like Healthy Boy Brand Mushroom Soy. In general, use the Japanese brand for Korean or Japanese dishes and the Superior Soy for Chinese dishes.

Spices

I always buy whole spices and grind them myself in a clean coffee grinder. Whole spices last longer and their flavors are much more intense. A basic Asian spice shelf should contain the following: black mustard seeds, black cardamom seeds, cayenne pepper, cinnamon stick, whole cloves, coriander seeds, cumin seeds, fennel seeds, Madras curry powder, paprika, peppercorns (black and white), kosher salt and table salt, raw sesame seeds, star anise, Szechuan peppercorns, and ground turmeric. Most of these spices are available in grocery stores. Szechuan peppercorns, black mustard seeds, and black cardamom seeds are available from Asian grocers, Indian grocers, spice shops or by mail order. See separate entries for garam masala, five-spice powder, and Szechuan peppercorns.

Tofu and Deep-Fried Tofu

Tofu, made from soy milk curds, is an excellent source of protein, available in sealed 15-ounce tubs. To drain tofu before cooking, wrap it in paper towels and put it in a bowl. Put some sort of weight on top, either a heavy plate or bowl, and pour off the liquid as it accumulates in the bowl. Draining takes about thirty minutes.

For frying, always buy firm tofu. If you buy it fresh, floating in tubs of water, it will need less time to drain. As with all tofu, if you don't use it up after opening the tub, put the extra in a bowl of fresh water to cover in the refrigerator. Do the same with the kind bought in Asian markets, changing the water daily. It will last three or four days this way.

Deep-fried tofu adds a chewy savoriness to Asian salads

and stir-fries. You can buy it pre-fried in Asian stores, but homemade tastes better. To deep-fry, slice the block into ¾-inch-wide pieces after draining. Heat canola oil in a deep-fryer or 2 cups of oil in a small skillet over medium heat. When the oil is completely hot, gently slide the tofu in, a few pieces at a time. Fry until golden brown and floating on the top, 3 to 5 minutes. Drain on a paper towel. Then further slice as described in the recipe.

Vinegar

I use five types of vinegar, all but one of which are available in grocery stores. For the recipes in this book, you need white distilled vinegar, Japanese rice vinegar (Mitsukan brand, not the seasoned variety), red wine vinegar, balsamic vinegar, and Chinese black vinegar (Gold Plum brand Chinkiang). You can use balsamic vinegar instead of the black vinegar, which may be hard to find.

Wakame

There are several types of dried seaweed, but I find wakame the easiest and tastiest to use in salads and miso soup. It usually comes in small pieces in 1-ounce plastic bags, so there's no need to cut it. To reconstitute, pour warm water over it and let it sit for twenty to thirty minutes, then squeeze out the excess moisture. However, there may be hard stems, so cut them off. Wakame is a Japanese product available by mail order, in Japanese markets, in some grocery stores, and in health food stores.

Equipment

the following are the few items that I use repeatedly when cooking Asian food. I assume that you have measuring cups and spoons, mixing bowls, a colander, salad spinner, and the like.

Coffee Grinder

I have a separate coffee grinder that I use exclusively for grinding spices such as fresh five-spice powder, garam masala, and other spice blends, peppercorns, and roasted spices. The flavor of these spices when freshly ground is so sharp and alive that, to my mind, doing it yourself is indispensible. Wet ingredients are best handled in a mortar with a pestle or food processor—they will break a coffee grinder (I have broken several). Use a mortar and pestle for dry spices as well—most people in Asia do—but doing so requires some finesse and practice. A grinder costs less than twenty dollars, so it's a small, worthwhile investment. Braun and Krupps are good brands.

Deep-Fryer

I can't say enough good things about deep-fryers. I bought one a few years ago and now I wonder how I managed without it for all those years. They confine the mess, the oil can be reused, and the temperature is always just right. I paid about twenty dollars for mine and use it for French fries, chicken wings, tofu, spring rolls, and fish cakes.

Food Processor

A small food processor is a necessity for the home cook. They are great for chopping peanuts, making spice pastes and pesto, grating carrots, mincing fish for fish cakes, or making your own ground pork. The 1-quart models don't take up much counter space and are powerful enough to do a good job.

Grill or Grill Pan

If you are lucky enough to have outdoor space, you should own a grill. I use a Weber kettle grill with charcoal, but anything from a tiny hibachi to a large gas-fired grill will do.

I also love grilling indoors in a grill pan. Even though I have an outdoor grill, I prefer to use the grill pan for certain jobs. It is great for vegetables like asparagus, sliced eggplant, and sweet potatoes that are difficult to do on the outdoor grill, and for fish fillets, lean meats, and boneless chicken breasts. Fatty meat produces too much grease and smoke for a grill pan, and chicken with the bone is too thick to cook properly. I prefer the anodized aluminum nonstick ones to cast-iron ones because they are much lighter and food doesn't stick as much. They come in round and square shapes—the difference is a matter of personal preference.

Grilling Basket

A wire grilling basket for an outdoor grill simplifies a cook's life, especially for turning fish and seafood without sticking, and vegetables are not lost to the fire.

Juicer

Lemon and lime juice are used frequently in Asian cooking. Any juicer will do—a simple plastic or glass juicer, the wooden handheld variety that you turn inside the fruit, or a fancy electric one. I just use my hands: plunge four clean fingers into a halved fruit over a bowl and work them around until all the juice is out. Be sure to remove any stray seeds.

Knives

If I had only one knife in the kitchen, it would be a six-inch chef's knife. It is totally all-purpose. You can cut up a whole chicken, julienne vegetables, slice onions, mince ginger and garlic, cut tomatoes, thinly slice meat—do almost anything. Beyond this jack-of-all-trades, it is nice to have a serrated knife, a paring knife, a cleaver, and maybe a carving knife. The chef's knife could do the job of all those knives except the cleaver. If you do a lot of chopping through the bone, get a cleaver, which makes the otherwise messy task of hacking up a cooked duck or chicken, or cutting spareribs into smaller pieces, the work of a moment.

You must keep your knives sharp. A sharpening stone is inexpensive. I wet it and run the edge of the blade over it on both sides on almost a daily basis. I have to do this because I just throw my knives in the drawer. A wooden block will help knives keep their edge so that you can go longer between sharpenings.

Mortar and Pestle

To combine dry spices with wet ingredients—peppercorns with cilantro root, garlic with salt, or lime segments with sugar—as is often done in Asian cooking, a mortar and pestle is the best choice. In Asia, a mortar or grinding stone is indispensible. A granite mortar and pestle is the easiest to use but also the most expensive. If not granite, purchase a marble or porcelain one. The trick is to develop your own style while trying to maintain a pounding-while-grinding action, yet not allowing ingredients to escape from the bowl.

Pots and Pans

A 3-quart chef's pan or sauté pan is essential. Use it instead of a wok. Because of the extreme slope of their sides, woks require higher temperatures than the average home stove-top can generate. I use my 3-quart chef's pan for most all stir-frying, stewing, sauce making, and braising. Substitute a 12-inch frying pan. For frying a whole fish or for a large stir-fry with a lot of noodles, a 5-quart sauté pan is also useful. You also should have a big stock pot for cooking noodles. The more room noodles have in a pot, the happier they are.

Rice Cooker

Rice cookers take the mystery out of cooking rice: it comes out perfect every time. The best ones are the electric, Japanese-made, vacuum-type cooker and warmer. They cost a hundred dollars and up, which is a lot, but they last a long time and are very convenient. I got mine while I was living in Japan in 1986, and it is still going strong. Put in as much rice as you want, then add water so that the water is one knuckle level higher than the rice. Close it up, turn it on, and wait for the light that tells you the rice is done. The cooker also keeps the rice warm after it is done, so you needn't time it perfectly with the rest of the meal. Rice cookers are designed for Japanese families, who eat rice at every meal. They simply make one large batch of rice in the morning, and the cooker keeps it warm and ready all day. I recommend the five- or ten-cup models.

If you don't want to spring for the expensive type of cooker I recommend, don't buy one of the other cheaper ones. You're better off just using a saucepan with a tight lid and following the one knuckle rule explained above.

Tongs and Utensils

I recommend having a long and a short tongs: the short for combining salads and noodles, and the long for grilling and cooking big pots of noodles. A set of wooden cooking tools is also indispensable.

Appetizers
and Salads

Meals in Asia have a different structure than in Western countries. Southeast Asian cooks tend to serve everything together—soup, salad, curries, vegetables, grilled items, sauces, pickles, and condiments—often at room temperature, usually centered around a bowl of rice. Eating is communal and leisurely. This style of presentation has a lot to do with the climate: these are tropical countries, and the heat and humidity make the idea of eating large, entree-sized portions less appealing. Diners in these countries prefer many small dishes, essentially as flavorings for rice. Strong flavors, variety, and different textures are presented to stimulate the appetite. What we think of as appetizers is streetfood in these countries, food to be eaten on the run or when alone.

Moving north to Japan and China, presentation changes. *Nomiya*, traditional Japanese pubs that specialize in sake and regional tidbits, are in fact stylish little temples devoted to the art of Japanese appetizers. It is considered inappropriate to drink without eating something in a Japanese bar. If you don't automatically order a snack, something will be brought to your table anyway.

In China, of course, there is dim sum, with all its delightful dumplings and other small plates of appetizers you pluck from passing restaurant carts and make a meal out of. There is also the ultimate in Chinese cooking, the banquet meal, where you may be served as many as thirty dishes, course after course.

Serving a small first course before a large entree is more of a Western concept than an Asian one. It works well for us, allowing us to spend a little more time at the table with family and friends. People are willing to eat more adventurously when it comes to appetizers. A deep-fried food or a sparerib will be ordered in a restaurant as an appetizer much more often than as an entree because it is seen as only a small indulgence. My favorite appetizers are deep-fried morsels like chicken wings dipped in tangy sauces, savory salads, and flavorful soups.

Spicy Chicken Wings

Chicken wings are the all-American appetizer, but here they are made distinctive with Asian spicing in this two-peppercorn, light batter mixture. While the recipe doesn't call for a dipping sauce, you could use the cilantro sauce on page 46 or the grilled vegetable dipping sauce on page 174. People shy away from making chicken wings at home because of the deep-frying, but they are delicious and fairly easy, especially if you have a fryer. However, a pot of oil on the stove works well and you can strain the oil and keep it in the refrigerator for quite some time. In my view, the only bad wing is an underdone wing, so test the first one to make sure it is cooked through and crispy on the outside. Buy small wings. Roaster wings are too big for even cooking and not appropriate for an appetizer.

Serve these before Pad Thai (page 100).

Serves 4

2½ pounds chicken wings

2 teaspoons Szechuan peppercorns

1 teaspoon black peppercorns

1 dried red chile

½ teaspoon kosher salt

¼ cup soy sauce

¼ cup rice wine

¼ cup flour

2 tablespoons cornstarch

Canola oil for deep-frying

Lemon wedges

1. Cut off the wing tips and then cut each wing into two pieces at the joint. Put them in a large bowl.

2. Toast the Szechuan peppercorns in a dry frying pan over medium-high heat until fragrant and just starting to smoke, 3 to 5 minutes. Grind them with the black peppercorns and red chile in a clean coffee grinder or mortar.

3. Combine the pepper mixture with the salt, soy sauce, rice wine, flour, and cornstarch in a small bowl. Stir until there are no lumps. Add this mixture to the wings and make sure each wing is well coated.

4. Heat 4 cups of oil over medium-high heat in a saucepan or preheat a deep-fryer and fry the wings (three to five at a time) until well browned and floating on the surface.

5. Arrange the wings on a serving platter and garnish with lemon wedges. Have a bottle of sriracha chili sauce on the side.

Fresh Spring Rolls with Peanut-Hoisin Sauce

People tend to be impressed by any kind of spring roll served at home—they have about them an aura of complexity. These are very simple, very fresh, and satisfying, especially with the traditional Vietnamese bean sauce served with uncooked spring rolls. Make them close to serving time and cover with a damp paper towel at room temperature until they are served, or they will dry out.

PEANUT-HOISIN SAUCE

2 tablespoons canola oil

½ small onion, minced

2 garlic cloves, minced

2 tablespoons creamy peanut butter

1 tablespoon hoisin sauce

1 tablespoon tomato paste

1 teaspoon sambal olek

2 teaspoons sugar

24 medium shrimp

Juice of ½ lime

Freshly ground black pepper

Kosher salt

24 circular 6-inch rice papers (plus extras for mistakes)

24 mint leaves

24 Thai basil leaves

2 scallions, cut into 2-inch lengths and julienned

1 jalapeño, thinly sliced into rings

Makes 24 pieces to serve 4 to 6

1. To make the dressing, heat the oil in a small saucepan and add the onion and garlic. Sauté for 5 to 8 minutes, or until the onion is transparent. Add ½ cup water along with the peanut butter, hoisin sauce, tomato paste, sambal olek, and sugar. Stir well and simmer for 5 minutes. Set the sauce aside to cool while you assemble the spring rolls.

2. Poach the shrimp in a small saucepan of gently simmering water until they curl and turn pink, about 30 seconds. Drain and refresh them with cold water. Put the shrimp in a small bowl and squeeze the lime juice over them, along with a liberal grinding of pepper and a sprinkling of salt.

3. Prepare your work area. Put all the ingredients in front of you along with a bowl of medium hot water and a serving platter. Dip the rice paper briefly into the water and place it on the work surface.

4. Straighten a shrimp by bending it backward until it snaps and place it horizontally in the bottom middle of the rice paper. Put one mint leaf, one basil leaf, and a few scallion shreds on top of the shrimp. Fold the bottom flap over the shrimp, fold the two sides in, and roll up.

5. Place the spring roll on the serving plate folded side down and cover the plate with a damp paper towel. Make the remaining 23 rolls in the same manner. Rice paper is very delicate; if you tear one, just toss it and start over.

6. Keep the rolls covered with the towel until you are ready to serve. Transfer the sauce to a small serving bowl and serve with a spoon so each diner can spoon the sauce over their rolls. If it has become quite thick, thin it with a tablespoon of water. Serve the jalapeño on a small plate on the side.

Chile Mussels

When you think of mussels, Belgian, French, or even Italian preparations come to mind, but this zesty, aromatic, and savory dish with Indian spices holds its own. Serve as a first course before Pepper-Marinated Salmon (page 112) or as a light lunch with a loaf of crusty bread. Now that farm-raised mussels are available almost everywhere, and they are pretty much free of grit, serving mussels at home is a nice option. Make sure the mussel shells are tightly closed once you put them in the bowl of water, and discard any that feel heavy. Buy extra so that you have two pounds after some are discarded. This dish can also be made with small clams.

Serves 4

2 pounds mussels, scrubbed and
    debearded
4 tablespoons canola oil
1 large onion, chopped
2 large garlic cloves, minced
1 tablespoon chopped ginger
1 large tomato or 3 plum tomatoes, chopped
2 dried red chiles
1 teaspoon turmeric
1 teaspoon paprika
½ cup chicken stock
1 teaspoon salt
Juice of 1 lemon
½ cup cilantro leaves

1. Soak the mussels in a large bowl of cool water for an hour. Discard any open mussels that don't close tightly when you pinch them between your fingers.

2. Heat the oil over medium heat in a pot (with a lid) large enough to hold all the mussels. When it's hot, add the onion, garlic, and ginger. Sauté until soft, about 5 minutes. Add the tomato and continue to sauté for 5 minutes. Break the chiles into pieces and add them to the onion mixture along with the turmeric and paprika. Cook the spices while stirring for 2 to 3 minutes. Add the chicken stock and salt, stir well, cover, and simmer for 3 minutes. You can make the recipe to this point up to 2 hours in advance.

3. Ten minutes before you want to serve, bring the sauce back to a boil and add the drained mussels. Cover at once and steam until all the shells are open, about 5 minutes. Remove the pot from the heat, add the lemon juice and cilantro leaves, and stir to mix.

4. Transfer the mussels to a large platter or bowl, discarding any mussels that don't open. Ladle the mussels into individual bowls and make sure there is an empty bowl on the side for shells.

Salt and Pepper Soft-Shell Crabs

Each year I await soft-shell crab season (which begins with the first full moon in May and runs through the summer) with great anticipation. Maryland blue crabs are plucked from the waters as they molt, or shed their hard shells, so you can eat the entire crab, legs and all. Because harvesting soft-shell crabs is not easy (they molt several times over the summer but must be taken from the water right after the shell has been shed), they are expensive and quite rich, so I serve them as an appetizer. Make sure you ask the fishmonger to clean the crabs—it is a tricky business. In Asian restaurants, they are usually deep-fried, but I shallow-fry them with garlic once they are dusted with seasoned cornstarch, then dip them in ginger sauce. As the meat of a soft-shell crab is so sweet, I don't think it needs the sugar that is customarily in the recipe.

Serve these before Lemongrass Pork Chops (page 122) for an elegant and relatively simple meal.

Ginger Sauce (page 114)

Serves 4

½ cup cornstarch

2 teaspoons kosher salt

1½ teaspoons freshly ground black or white pepper

4 soft-shell crabs, cleaned, washed, and patted dry with paper towels

½ cup canola oil

2 garlic cloves, minced

2 cups shredded red leaf or romaine lettuce

1. Make the Ginger Sauce and set aside in a small serving bowl.

2. Combine the cornstarch, salt, and pepper on a plate and shake the plate to mix evenly. Dust each crab well with the mixture and shake off any excess. (This should be done just as the oil is heating.)

3. Heat the oil over medium-high heat in a frying pan large enough to hold the crabs comfortably in a single layer. When the oil is hot, add the garlic and stir-fry it for 30 seconds. Add the crabs. Cook the first side for 2 to 3 minutes and flip them. They should be deep orange and crispy. Cook the other side for 2 to 3 minutes. Cover a serving platter with the shredded lettuce and top with the crabs. Serve the Ginger Sauce on the side.

Japanese Salt-Grilled Fish

In Japan there is no such thing as a "Japanese restaurant." Each establishment specializes in a particular type of food, serving only sushi or only soba, or what have you. One of my favorites is the *robatayaki*. If you think teppanyaki-style restaurants like Benihana are lively, a *robatayaki* takes the atmosphere to another level. The cooks and waiters wear regional costumes and engage in ongoing banter, with good-natured yelling of orders, welcoming of guests, and flamboyant behavior all around. The cooking is centered around a large grill pit (*robatayaki* means "grilled by the fireside"), where fish, seafood, and other ingredients are skewered and placed standing up in the ashes and sand of the grill floor. My favorite is *sawagani*, tiny salt-grilled crabs. You just pop the entire crab in your mouth—the flavor and crunch are fabulous, as is the round of cheers and *"sawagani!"* chants you will hear from the waiters and cooks.

I use whole trout for this salt-grilled fish, or *shioyaki*, because it is the only small whole fish that I see consistently in grocery store fish departments. Try the recipe with mackerel if it is available. Ask the fishmonger to bone the fish for you while leaving the skin, head, and tail intact for easy eating.

Serve this first course before Japanese Yakisoba (page 96).

Serves 4

DIPPING SAUCE

½ cup unseasoned rice vinegar

¼ cup soy sauce

1 cup dashi (see page 11)

4 whole trout (¾ pound each), washed and patted dry

2 tablespoons kosher salt

Lemon wedges

*Everyday
Asian*

1. Combine the vinegar, soy sauce, and dashi in a small saucepan and bring them to a simmer. Reduce the liquid by half and pour into a small serving bowl.

2. Coat the trout inside and out with the salt and place them on a platter.

3. Prepare your grill. With an outdoor grill, use a grill basket. If you don't have one, try to skewer them, two at a time with two metal skewers, so the skewers are vertical to the trout. If you are using a grill pan, coat it lightly with oil and you won't need any skewers. Grill the trout 3 to 5 minutes per side over high heat so that you have nice crisp skin.

4. Pour the dipping sauce into tiny bowls, if you have them, and give one to each guest. Serve with lemon wedges.

Fried Oysters with Cilantro Sauce

Deep-fried morsels like these oysters are wonderful with this tangy cilantro condiment. The same sauce could be used with deep-fried shrimp, chicken wings, or spring rolls. The oysters go well before most any noodle entree. Buy shucked oysters for this recipe and get them as large as you can. Some of the cornmeal coating will come off in the frying process, so instead of using a deep-fryer, which would require an oil change after one use, I fry these in a deep-frying pan.

Serves 4

CILANTRO SAUCE

1 bunch cilantro

Juice of 1 lime

1 teaspoon sambal olek

½ teaspoon salt

1 tablespoon rice wine

1 pound shucked oysters (12 to 18)

½ cup cornmeal

½ cup flour

½ teaspoon salt

½ teaspoon freshly ground pepper

Canola oil for shallow-frying

1. To make the sauce, finely chop the cilantro in a food processor or blender. Combine it with the lime juice, sambal olek, and salt in a small bowl. Stir to mix and set aside. It will become more of a sauce as the moisture comes out of the cilantro.

2. Add the rice wine to the oysters and let them sit in a colander for 15 minutes. Combine the cornmeal, flour, salt, and pepper in a medium bowl. Toss the oysters in the cornstarch mixture and make sure each one is well coated.

3. Heat ½ inch oil in a medium frying pan over medium-high heat. When the oil is hot (test it with a drop of water—if it hisses right back, it is ready), shake the excess flour from an oyster and gently drop it into the oil. Cook as many at a time as will comfortably fit in the pan. Flip them after 30 seconds. They should be brown and crispy. Cook the other side for 30 seconds. Remove the oysters with a slotted spoon and drain them on a paper towel. Try to cook them in just two batches so they will stay hot.

4. Serve immediately with the cilantro sauce. Place the oysters around the edge of a small round serving plate with a smaller bowl of the bright green sauce in the middle.

Roasted Asparagus with Miso Dressing

Serve this versatile dish with almost anything, or let it stand alone as a first course. Miso goes well with the flavor of asparagus and is a nice change from a standard vinaigrette. I experimented a lot with grilling asparagus in a grill pan versus roasting them in the oven—oven roasting cooks them much more evenly. In Japan, this would be served as the *sunomono* or "vinegared things" course. The dressing could also be served on a green salad. Try this before Burmese Chicken Coconut Curry (page 142) or alongside Thai Grilled Chicken (page 110).

Serves 4

1½ pounds asparagus
1 tablespoon canola oil
Salt

MISO DRESSING
3 tablespoons unseasoned rice vinegar
2 tablespoons light miso
2 teaspoons sesame oil
1 teaspoon sugar

1. Preheat the oven to 375°F. Cut the bottom inch off the asparagus stalks; with a vegetable peeler, peel the bottom 4 inches of each stalk. Lay the stalks in a single layer in a roasting pan, sprinkle with the oil, and salt them lightly. Roast for 20 to 30 minutes or until they are cooked through but not mushy. Shake the pan every 10 minutes. Remove them to a serving plate to cool.

2. Make the dressing by combining the ingredients with 2 tablespoons water. Stir to dissolve the sugar and miso.

3. When the asparagus is cool, pour the dressing over it and allow the salad to sit for 15 minutes before serving.

Indonesian Gado Gado

The island of Bali is my vacation destination of choice. The people are beautiful, proud of their culture, extremely artistic, and friendly in an easygoing way. Their food reflects this. On our last trip, I tried to write down details about the dishes I ate so that I could re-create them at home, but the ingredients that are commonplace there— rhizomes like *kencur* and *laos,* salam and pandan leaf for aromatics, fruits such as rambutans and mangosteens—are impossible to find here. Gado gado, a vegetable salad with a warm peanut dressing, is one Indonesian dish that you can do justice to with readily available ingredients. Krupah, fried shrimp crackers, add a nice crunch if you can find them. In Indonesia, a sliced hard-boiled egg or a fried egg is placed on top, but I prefer it without. Serve this salad Bali-style with rice, as a meal, or before the Five-Spice Game Hens (page 106).

Serves 4 to 6

PEANUT DRESSING

1 tablespoon canola or peanut oil

1 large garlic clove, minced

½ small onion, minced

½ teaspoon dried shrimp paste

1 tablespoon light brown sugar

½ cup smooth peanut butter

½ cup coconut milk

1 tablespoon soy sauce

1 tablespoon fish sauce

¼ teaspoon cayenne pepper, or more to taste

Juice of ½ lime

2 large carrots, grated

½ head Savoy cabbage (1 pound), thinly sliced

4 cups mixed salad greens

½ pound green beans, blanched and cut into 1-inch pieces

2 large red potatoes, boiled, cooled, and cut into 1-inch cubes

1 cucumber, skin on, scored vertically all the way around
  with the tines of a fork and sliced into thin rounds

8 ounces deep-fried tofu (see page 27), cut into
  ¼-inch-thick strips

1 cup crispy fried onions (see 9)

10 krupah (optional)

Cilantro sprigs for garnish

Lime wedges for garnish

1. To make the dressing, heat the oil in a small saucepan over medium heat. Add the garlic and onion and fry until soft, about 5 minutes. Add the shrimp paste, crushing it with the back of a fork while frying for a minute. Add the brown sugar, peanut butter, coconut milk, ⅔ cup water, soy sauce, fish sauce, and pepper. Stir until all the ingredients are well combined. Bring to a simmer and allow to thicken while stirring, 3 to 5 minutes. It should be the consistency of a creamy dressing. Remove the peanut sauce from the heat and stir in the lime juice.

2. To assemble the salad, toss the carrots, cabbage, and salad greens together in a mixing bowl, then spread on a platter. Sprinkle the green beans over the cabbage mixture. Place the potatoes around the edge of the platter. Arrange the cucumber slices around the platter beside the potatoes. Mound the tofu strips in the center.

3. Spoon the still warm dressing over the salad in a large circle. Sprinkle the crispy fried onions over the top and place the krupah in a circle inside the cucumber slices. Garnish further with the cilantro sprigs and lime wedges.

Burmese Fish Cake Salad

You can buy prepared fish cakes in Asian markets, but those made at home have an infinitely better consistency. Fish cakes should have a chewy texture, which you get by finely grinding the fish and adding egg and cornstarch. This salad showcases fish cakes together with the contrasting textures of potatoes, greens, and crispy fried onions. The dressing for the salad is a savory, all-purpose one—try serving it on a salade Niçoise.

Make this salad as a first course for any of the noodle soups in this book. On a recent fall weekend we had friends out for a long hike in the country, and afterward I served this salad followed by Vietnamese Beef Pho. Together, they made for a meal that was hearty without being too heavy.

Serves 4

FISH CAKES

1 pound fillets of flounder or similar
    mild white-fleshed fish

1½ tablespoons fish sauce

1 teaspoon red curry paste

1 egg, beaten

2 tablespoons cornstarch

2 thick slices red onion, finely chopped

SALAD DRESSING

2 tablespoons fish sauce

Juice of 2 limes

2 tablespoons dried shrimp powder

2 tablespoons oil from crispy fried onions
    (see page 9)

5 cups mixed salad greens (such as arugula and red leaf)

4 medium red potatoes, boiled, cooled, and cut into 1-inch cubes

4 large radishes, thinly sliced

Canola oil for deep-frying

1 cup crispy fried onions (see page 9)

1. Pat the fish fillets with paper towels to make sure they are as dry as possible. Cut the fish into chunks and process in a food processor or blender until the fish forms a paste. Add the fish sauce, curry paste, egg, and cornstarch to the fish mixture. Process again until everything is well combined. Use a spatula to transfer the mixture to a bowl and stir in the red onion. Form the batter into small, flat patties 2½ inches in diameter. The fish cakes will be quite sticky, so place them on a plate in the refrigerator until you are ready to cook them.

2. Combine the dressing ingredients in a small bowl. Mix well, and set aside.

3. Cover a large platter with the mixed greens. Place the potatoes around the edge. Scatter the radishes over the potatoes. Refrigerate the platter.

4. Heat the oil in a deep-fryer or pour ½-inch deep in a frying pan for shallow-frying over medium-high heat. When the oil's hot, slip in a few fish cakes at a time. They will be nicely browned and float to the surface of a deep-fryer in about 3 minutes. If shallow-frying, flip them after 1½ minutes in the pan. Cook the other side for 1½ minutes and remove to a paper towel to drain.

5. Slice each fish cake into four pieces and scatter them on top of the salad. They're best if served warm. Top with all the dressing and the crispy fried onions.

Vietnamese Cabbage, Chicken, and Mint Salad

This well-known Vietnamese salad appears on most menus as *goi ga bap cai*. I like to pickle the onions and chiles—it mellows the flavors. Many people aren't crazy about eating raw cabbage, so I sometimes use shredded romaine instead. The idea with this salad is to get the various ingredients roughly the same size and shape. It is really the Vietnamese version of coleslaw, but the flavors are much lighter and brighter. The chicken and peanuts add a substantial meatiness. It is a nice first course followed by any nonpoultry grilled entree.

Serves 4

½ cup raw peanuts

¼ cup white distilled vinegar

½ small red onion, thinly sliced

½ serrano chile, or more to taste, thinly sliced into rings

1 pound boneless, skinless chicken breasts

¼ cup fish sauce

Juice of 1 lime

2 tablespoons sugar

½ head Savoy cabbage (1 pound), thinly sliced

3 carrots, grated

1 small bunch mint, leaves rolled up and julienned, plus
    sprigs for garnish

1. Toast the peanuts in an oven or toaster oven at 350°F until golden brown, 10 to 15 minutes. Cool and chop coarsely.

2. Combine the vinegar with the onion and chile in a small bowl. Let the mixture sit for 30 minutes.

3. Bring 3 cups of water to a boil in a frying pan, add the chicken, cover, lower the heat to a simmer, and poach the chicken until just done, about 10 minutes. Remove with a slotted spoon. Once the chicken breast has cooled, pull it by hand into thin strips.

4. Make the dressing by combining the fish sauce, lime juice, and sugar in a small bowl. Stir until the sugar is dissolved.

5. Combine the cabbage, chicken, carrots, mint, vinegar-onion mixture, dressing, and peanuts in a large bowl. Toss thoroughly and transfer to a serving platter. Garnish with a few sprigs of mint.

Seaweed Salad with Tofu and Sprouts

This is a savory Japanese-style seaweed salad. Wakame has the best flavor but try other commonly available dried seaweeds, such as hijiki or kombu. (Kombu has to be sliced after being reconstituted.) Do not use nori, which is the thin laver used to wrap sushi rolls—it is eaten only in the dried form, which isn't right for this salad. Wakame comes dried and needs to be soaked in water for twenty to thirty minutes. It adds a nice chewiness, deep green color, and sea taste to a salad. Deep-fried tofu makes this salad more substantial and adds a contrasting texture.

Serve as a first course before the Grilled Striped Bass with Ginger Sauce (page 114).

¼ cup dried wakame

Serves 4

DRESSING

¼ cup sesame seeds

3 tablespoons unseasoned rice vinegar

2 tablespoons soy sauce

2 teaspoons sugar

1 teaspoon sesame oil

10 ounces deep-fried tofu (see page 27), cut into
  ¼-inch-thick slices

2 ounces alfalfa or broccoli sprouts

1 cucumber, peeled, scored vertically all around with the
  tines of a fork, and sliced into thin circles

1. Soak the wakame in a bowl of tepid water for 20 minutes until soft. Drain it in a colander and squeeze in a paper towel.

2. To make the dressing, toast the sesame seeds in a dry frying pan over medium heat until they are golden brown, shaking the pan as they cook, about 5 minutes. Cool and grind them in a clean coffee grinder for just a few pulses.

3. Put the ground seeds in a small bowl and add the rice vinegar, soy sauce, sugar, and sesame oil. Stir to mix. Set the dressing aside while you assemble the salad.

4. Combine the tofu, wakame, and sprouts in a mixing bowl. Add all of the dressing and combine thoroughly with tongs. Lay the cucumbers around the edge of a small serving plate and heap the salad in the middle.

Cucumber Salad with Dried Shrimp and Peanuts

A *yum* is a classic Thai salad with several different textures. The cucumbers add crunch, the shrimp have a chewy sweetness, and the peanuts provide a meaty element. Chiles, lime juice, and fish sauce give the whole thing flavor and freshness. I like to serve this with Roast Chicken with Szechuan Peppercorns (page 144).

Serves 4

⅓ cup raw peanuts

2 large cucumbers

¼ cup dried shrimp, soaked in a cup of water for 15 minutes
and coarsely chopped, or 2 tablespoons dried shrimp powder

1 serrano chile, thinly sliced into rings

Two ¼-inch-thick slices red onion, chopped into small pieces

2 tablespoons chopped cilantro leaves

1 tablespoon canola oil

Juice of 1 lime

2 tablespoons fish sauce

2 teaspoons sugar

1. Toast the peanuts in a 350°F oven or toaster oven until golden brown, 10 to 15 minutes. Chop them coarsely.

2. Peel the cucumbers and cut them in half lengthwise. Scoop the seeds out with a spoon and slice into ¼-inch-thick half-moons.

3. Combine the cucumbers and peanuts with the dried shrimp, chile, onion, cilantro, oil, lime juice, fish sauce, and sugar. Mix well.

4. Let the salad sit for 30 minutes before serving to let the flavors meld; allow the cucumbers to release some of their water.

Arugula Salad with Deep-Fried Tofu

Arugula has character. Thanks to its spinach-like texture and its spicy, peppery flavor, it holds up well to a soy sauce–based dressing. Tofu, the other primary ingredient in this dish, has multiple personalities. If you know it only in its fresh form—soft and creamy—you'll find that when deep-fried, tofu becomes earthy, savory, meaty but light. These two ingredients are the perfect foil for one another. Serve with Five-Spice Game Hens (page 106), Indian Spice–Rubbed Pork Chops (page 105), or Roast Chicken with Szechuan Peppercorns (page 144).

Serves 4

1 large bunch arugula (8 ounces)

8 ounces deep-fried tofu, sliced into ¼-inch-thick pieces
(see page 27)

SALAD DRESSING

2 tablespoons soy sauce

1 teaspoon sesame oil

1 teaspoon sugar

2 tablespoons unseasoned rice vinegar

1 teaspoon balsamic vinegar

2 teaspoons finely chopped ginger

1. Soak the arugula in a large bowl of water, then spin it dry. It is a dirty green, so taste to see if it needs a second soaking. Tear the arugula into pieces and put it in a medium bowl along with the fried tofu.

2. To make the dressing, combine the dressing ingredients in a small bowl. Stir to dissolve the sugar. Add the dressing to the arugula mixture and toss well. Transfer to a serving bowl.

Thai Nam Prik with Crudités

Nam prik, or chile water, is a sauce that is somewhere between an Indonesian sambal, or chile-fried condiment, and a dipping sauce like Vietnamese nuoc cham. I think of it as the adhesive that brings the various dishes together in a Thai meal. Nam prik takes many forms, from thin to chunky, and the ingredients can vary tremendously, but it always contains something sour, something salty, something sweet, and of course, the chiles. And it is always intense. If all you had was a bowl of rice and nam prik, you could call it a meal. Entire chapters of Thai cookbooks are devoted to this elemental sauce. Mine is a basic version—a great condiment for vegetables that completes a meal. Serve it with plenty of jasmine rice and Thai Grilled Chicken (page 110).

As Thais are master vegetable carvers, their platters would be filled with cucumber leaves, radish flowers, scallion curls, and the like. Cut the vegetables into interesting shapes if you like. I suggest using papaya in this dish, but if you can't find it, use slightly underripe melon or mango or leave the fruit out altogether.

Serves 4

NAM PRIK

¼ cup dried shrimp, soaked in a bowl of water
    for 15 minutes, drained, and chopped

Juice of 1 lime

¼ cup fish sauce

1 serrano chile, thinly sliced into rings

¼ small red onion or 2 shallots, finely chopped

¼ cup cilantro leaves

1 tablespoon sugar

¼ pound tender green beans, blanched in boiling water for
    5 minutes, drained, and rinsed in cold water

1 cucumber, peeled and sliced into ¼-inch-thick rounds

2 carrots, cut into thin 3-inch-long sticks

5 large radishes, sliced

⅓ papaya, peeled and cut into sticks (it is best if the papaya
is slightly underripe)

1. Make the nam prik by combining the dried shrimp, lime juice, fish sauce, chile, red onion, cilantro, and sugar in a small serving bowl. Stir to dissolve the sugar.

2. Prepare a platter of vegetables and fruit by grouping each type together. Serve with the bowl of dipping sauce in the center with a spoon.

Tossed Salad with Lemon-Ginger Dressing

So simple, but this salad always brings a little smile of pleased surprise. It was the house salad at my restaurant, and customers constantly asked me for the dressing recipe. Serve it with an Asian meal instead of a salad with the usual olive oil and vinegar dressing. It is oil free, light, and tangy and goes equally well with fried food, cold noodles, or a barbecue.

DRESSING

Serves 4

3 tablespoons unseasoned rice vinegar

2 tablespoons lemon juice

1 teaspoon minced ginger

1 tablespoon sugar

¼ teaspoon salt

½ cucumber, peeled and thinly sliced into rounds

1 head red leaf lettuce, or romaine, leaves torn
    into small pieces

1 carrot, grated

4 thin slices red onion

1. Make the dressing by combining the dressing ingredients in a small bowl. Stir to dissolve the sugar.

2. Place the cucumber slices in a bowl and pour the dressing over them. Let them marinate for 15 minutes.

3. Combine the lettuce, carrot, and onion in a bowl and toss with tongs. Pour in the cucumbers and dressing and toss again. Transfer to a serving bowl.

Carrot and Mustard Seed Salad

On occasion a cook wants something that's not quite a side dish but is more than a garnish. This simple and subtle shredded carrot salad fills that role. It works well on a platter of grilled steaks or chicken (spread it around the edge of the platter and put your meat in the center) or with other vegetable dishes and rice. It is also nice on the same plate as a cold noodle salad. If you have a mandoline, use it, and you will have a very attractive salad with long delicate pieces.

Serves 4

5 medium or 3 large carrots

½ teaspoon salt

2 tablespoons unseasoned rice vinegar

2 tablespoons canola oil

1 tablespoon black mustard seeds

2 teaspoons sesame seeds

1. Shred the carrots with a grater, food processor, or mandoline. Put the carrot in a bowl, add the salt and vinegar, and toss with tongs.

2. Heat the oil in a small frying pan over medium heat; when it is hot, add the mustard and sesame seeds. As soon as they begin to pop, 2 to 3 minutes, pour the contents of the pan into the carrots. Toss again with tongs and refrigerate until you are ready to serve.

3. The flavor improves with at least an hour in the refrigerator.

Soups

Soup is a versatile mainstay of Asian cuisine. In Southeast Asia, it is served with the meal to provide liquid, since meals are often served without drinks and tea is drunk only after the meal. It is sold from carts in Singapore, Malaysia, Thailand, and Vietnam for breakfast, lunch, or between-meal snacks. In Japan, certain restaurants serve nothing else.

Soup can be a meal in a bowl, like the noodle soups in this chapter, or a little something to stimulate the appetite, like the miso or lemongrass soup. The soups in this chapter are mostly classics, each of which nicely represents the distinctive blend of flavors and ingredients in its national cuisine.

Miso Soup with Tofu and Wakame

Miso soup is one of the basic parts of Japanese daily life. I've read that three-quarters of the Japanese population starts the day with this soup, and some people consume it as many as three times a day. During our time in Japan we enjoyed staying at traditional Japanese inns called *ryokan*, which serve a Japanese breakfast on a low table set on the tatami mats of your room after the futons have been folded up. A traditional breakfast usually consists of broiled, partially dried fish, rice, pickles, and nourishing miso soup. Serve miso soup before Japanese Yakisoba (page 96), or try it for breakfast with a bowl of rice on the side. Try substituting reconstituted, thinly sliced Chinese mushrooms for the wakame. You can also experiment with different types of miso (see page 17).

Serves 4

1 tablespoon dried wakame

4 cups dashi (see page 11)

¼ cup red miso

¼ pound silk tofu, drained and cut into ½-inch cubes

2 scallions, thinly sliced into rounds

1. Reconstitute the seaweed by letting it sit in a small bowl with a cup of water for 30 minutes. Drain it, squeeze in a paper towel, and discard any hard pieces.

2. Heat the dashi over medium heat and add the miso. Stir until the miso is dissolved. The trick with miso is not to let it boil. It shouldn't really be cooked, just heated.

3. Add the tofu and wakame to the soup. Heat to a simmer and serve at once, garnished with the scallions. The soup should be very hot. Serve one ladleful to each person.

Vietnamese Beef Pho

Pho (pronounced fuh) is one of the world's most delicious soups; with a rich beef broth, rare steak, slithery rice noodles, and fresh herbs, the combination is perfect. Traditionally, the seasonings are individually added by the customer at the table. I served pho at my restaurant fully seasoned, with a sriracha chili sauce on the side for those who wanted more heat. A few Vietnam vets used to come especially for this soup and sit at the counter reminiscing about humid mornings in Saigon bent over a big bowl of pho. It is served throughout the day in Vietnam, especially at breakfast.

The beef must be thinly sliced, so that it cooks thoroughly in the hot broth. Place the beef in the freezer for an hour before you slice it. The all-important stock develops its intense flavor by long cooking; don't cheat on cooking time. The stock can be made ahead.

This soup is wonderful with a first course of Fresh Spring Rolls (page 38).

Serves 4

Soup Stock

1 large onion, unpeeled
3-inch piece ginger
3 pounds beef bones
3 whole star anise
2-inch cinnamon stick
1 pound stewing beef, brisket, or oxtails

⅓ cup fish sauce
¼ cup Chinese black vinegar, or balsamic vinegar
1 tablespoon chili sauce
¼ teaspoon freshly ground black pepper
¾ pound flank steak

10 ounces rice noodles, soaked in a bowl of water for 30
   minutes

2 cups mixed cilantro, mint, and Thai basil leaves

1 cup bean sprouts

2 jalapeño chiles, thinly sliced into rings

1 lime, sliced into wedges

1. Roast the whole onion and the ginger right on the oven rack in a 350°F oven for 30 minutes.

2. Put 3½ quarts of water, the bones, spices, onion, ginger, and stewing meat in a large soup pot and bring to a boil. Skim off any scum, lower the heat, and let cook at a medium simmer until reduced by one-third, about 3 hours. Strain the stock, reserving the stew meat.

3. Bring a large pot of water to a boil for the noodles. Skim the fat from the soup stock and add the fish sauce, black vinegar, chili sauce, and pepper. Bring the stock back to a simmer in a medium saucepan.

4. Slice the flank steak against the grain as thinly as possible. Cut the reserved stew meat into small cubes.

5. Drain the soaked noodles; boil for 2 minutes, drain, and rinse with cool water. Turn the heat up to high under the stock and let it come to a boil.

6. Divide the noodles, cubed beef, and sliced raw steak among four bowls. Pour the boiling stock into each bowl and top with a handful of herbs, bean sprouts, chiles, and a lime wedge. Serve at once.

7. If you want to serve from a large tureen at the table, toss the raw steak into the boiling broth for 30 seconds and pour over the noodles and stew meat in the tureen. (You won't be able to get the broth hot enough to cook the meat, otherwise.)

Lemongra*ss* Soup with Shrimp, Tomato, and Straw Mu*s*hroom*s*

Called *tom yum kung* in Thailand or *canh chua tom* in Vietnam, this is the fiery, hot and sour soup of Southeast Asia. I have it in every Thai or Vietnamese restaurant I visit in hopes of re-creating the experience of one fragrant bowl I had on the Thai island of Phuket, sitting on the beach, watching the sunset as tears streamed down my cheeks. It was all very beautiful, but the tears were, in fact, from the chiles. Even so, I couldn't stop eating that soup. I offer a lighter Vietnamese version without the Thai additions of chili paste or hard-to-get fresh galangal. This recipe is a simple, citrus-infused initiation into this classic soup. In Asia, the base is made from shrimp heads, which are rarely available here, so instead I use chicken stock flavored with shrimp shells. If you have dried lime leaves, this is a good use for them.

Serve this before Thai Beef Salad (page 118) or any grilled or roasted meat.

Serves 4

1 pound medium shrimp, peeled
   and deveined, tails left on and shells reserved

4½ cups unsalted homemade chicken stock

3 lemongrass stalks

4 kaffir lime leaves, or 2 strips of lime zest, julienned

One 15-ounce can straw mushrooms, drained

1 small tomato, sliced into small wedges

3 tablespoons fish sauce

3 tablespoons lime juice

½ serrano chile, or more to taste, thinly sliced into rings

Freshly ground black pepper

Cilantro sprigs for garnish

1. Put the shrimp shells and the chicken broth in a medium saucepan and boil for 5 minutes. Strain the broth and put it back in the pan.

2. Use only the bottom 6 inches of the lemongrass; chop off the green tops and the bulbous ends. Cut the stalks into 2-inch lengths and bruise them with the side of a wide knife, so that they remain intact but are somewhat flattened and release their fragrance.

3. Add the lemongrass, lime leaves, straw mushrooms, and tomato to the stock and simmer for 5 minutes.

4. Combine the fish sauce, lime juice, chile, and pepper in a small bowl and stir to mix. You can do this much up to an hour in advance; just turn the heat off and cover the pot on the stove.

5. Five minutes before you want to serve, heat the stock over medium-high heat; when it's hot, add the shrimp. As soon as they become pink and curl, 30 seconds to a minute, they are done. Quickly add the fish sauce mixture and stir to mix. Pour into a tureen and garnish with the cilantro sprigs. Serve at once.

Japanese Soba with Chicken and Mushrooms

While living in Japan, my husband and I spent our weekends exploring the backstreets and little neighborhoods of Tokyo. We would get off the train at a new stop each week and continue on foot throughout the afternoon. We would always stop for lunch at little family-run noodle shops for a bowl of ramen, soba, or udon. Those are some of the most pleasant food memories of my life. Coming through the cloth noren in the doorway to terrific smells, a few tiny tables or stools, and the cries of *"irashaimasen!"* ("welcome") was all very romantic.

Soup with soba noodles can be made quite simply at home. I make it with a traditional dashi and soy sauce broth, shiitake mushrooms, chicken breast, and spinach. I serve it for lunch if people are visiting for the day and I have a more elaborate dinner planned. It is also mild and soothing for someone who is feeling under the weather. And, of course, it's low in calories and fat. I have made mirin an optional ingredient—it adds a slight sweetness to the broth.

I would serve this dish by itself.

Serves 4

8 dried Chinese mushrooms or fresh
    shiitakes

¼ cup plus 2 tablespoons soy sauce

1 tablespoon minced ginger

1 tablespoon rice wine or sake

1 pound boneless, skinless chicken breasts, sliced into
    ¼-inch pieces

1 pound dried soba noodles

6 cups dashi (see page 11)

⅓ cup mirin (optional)

6 ounces spinach, cleaned and torn into small pieces

3 scallions, cut into 1-inch pieces on the diagonal

1. Soak the dried mushrooms in warm water for 30 minutes, drain, remove the hard stems, and slice the caps.

2. Combine the 2 tablespoons soy sauce with the ginger and rice wine in a medium bowl. Add the chicken to the bowl, coat well, and let marinate for 30 minutes.

3. Bring a large pot of water to a boil and cook the soba noodles until tender, 8 to 10 minutes. Drain the soba and rinse it with cold water.

4. Heat the dashi in a medium saucepan over medium heat. Add the ¼ cup soy sauce and the mirin if you are using it. Bring the broth to a simmer and add the chicken, spinach, and mushrooms. (If you are using fresh shiitakes, add them when you begin to heat the dashi.) Continue to cook until the chicken is white throughout and the spinach has wilted, 3 to 5 minutes.

5. You can serve this either in individual soup bowls or in a tureen. In either case, put the drained noodles in the bottom of the bowl and pour the hot soup over them. Garnish with the scallions and serve at once.

Chinese Cellophane Noodle and Pork Soup

I've been making this soup for twenty years, but I tend to forget about it until sometime in October when it starts to get cool and I want something substantial but healthy. The soup is a good use for cellophane noodles, as it becomes almost stew-like when the noodles cook in the broth and expand. No other noodle will do this without becoming mushy or pasty. If you are not a red meat eater, substitute shrimp for the pork; just add them for the last two minutes of cooking time. If you cannot find dried shrimp, make the soup without them, but they do add depth to the broth.

Serves 4

2 tablespoons canola oil

10 ounces napa cabbage or bok choy, sliced into
     2-inch square pieces

1 pound pork loin or pork chop meat, sliced into
     ½-inch pieces

1 heaping tablespoon dried shrimp or dried shrimp powder

2 quarts chicken stock

8 dried Chinese mushrooms

1½ teaspoons salt

3 tablespoons red wine vinegar

2 tablespoons soy sauce

3 ounces cellophane noodles, soaked in a bowl of
     warm water for 15 minutes, drained and
     cut into 6-inch lengths with scissors

1 tablespoon sesame oil

3 scallions, thinly sliced into rings

1. Soak the dried mushrooms in warm water for 30 minutes, drain, remove the hard stems, and slice the caps. Soak the dried shrimp in a bowl of water for 15 minutes, drain and chop.

2. Heat the oil in a large saucepan or chef's pan over medium heat. Add the cabbage and stir-fry until wilted, about 5 minutes. Add the pork and the dried shrimp and stir-fry until the pork changes color, about 2 minutes.

3. Add the chicken stock, mushrooms, salt, vinegar, and soy sauce to the pan. Bring to a simmer, cook for 5 minutes, and add the noodles. Bring the soup back to a simmer for 5 minutes longer while the noodles cook and become transparent. Add the sesame oil and stir to combine.

4. Pour the soup into a tureen and garnish with the scallions. Serve at once.

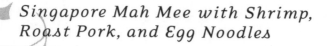

Singapore Mah Mee with Shrimp, Roast Pork, and Egg Noodles

Some of the best street food in the world is served at the "hawker" stands in Singapore. At these open-air restaurants, where many vendors gather and serve their specialties, you sample a variety of dishes from the main cuisines of the island nation—Chinese, Indian, Nonya, Indonesian, and Malay—eat at communal tables, and watch the dishes stack up. I always wondered how each stand got all of its dishes and cutlery back, but somehow the system works. I remember one memorable meal that my husband and I and our little daughter had on a hot August night. It included, among other things, three different kinds of noodle soup: one rich with coconut milk, one piquant, and one called "seven-plus noodles." We washed it all down with fresh starfruit juice and fresh green apple juice—it was heavenly. This soup is a Nonya dish. Nonyas are the Straits-born Malaysian wives of Straits Chinese men: the "marriage" makes for a wonderful cuisine, combining Chinese and Malaysian ingredients.

Serve this soup with a first course of Indonesian Gado Gado (page 50).

Serves 4

6 cups chicken stock

1 pound medium shrimp, peeled and deveined, shells reserved

2 tablespoons peanut or canola oil

1 tablespoon sesame oil

1 tablespoon chopped ginger

2 large garlic cloves, minced

2 scallions, chopped

8 ounces broccoli rabe, Chinese broccoli, or spinach, chopped into 2-inch pieces, bottom 2 inches of stem removed

2 teaspoons salt

½ teaspoon five-spice powder

10 ounces thin Chinese egg noodles

½ pound Chinese Roast Pork Tenderloin, thinly sliced
    (page 156)

Cilantro sprigs for garnish

1. Heat the chicken stock in a large saucepan over medium heat and add the shrimp shells and 1 cup water. Simmer the stock for 15 minutes and strain into a bowl.

2. In the same saucepan, heat the peanut and sesame oils over medium heat; add the ginger, garlic, and scallions. Stir-fry for 2 minutes. Add the broccoli rabe and sauté until the greens are wilted, 4 to 6 minutes. Add the stock, salt, and five-spice powder. Simmer for 10 minutes. Meanwhile, bring a large pot of water to a boil.

3. Boil the egg noodles, loosening the bundles with tongs, until just done, about 5 minutes. Drain and rinse with warm water. Shake the colander well and put the noodles in the bottom of a soup tureen.

4. Add the roast pork and raw shrimp to the simmering broth and cook until the shrimp turn pink and curl, about a minute.

5. Pour the hot broth over the noodles, garnish with the cilantro sprigs, and serve at once. You could also garnish this dish with crispy fried garlic or crispy fried onions (see page 9).

Southeast Asian Seafood Soup

This is the type of seafood soup I am always looking for at restaurants: one that is fresh, simple, and tastes of the sea. I often use an assortment of three kinds of shellfish such as lobster, scallops, and clams. Lobster shells flavor the broth, scallops provide meatiness, and clams give the soup the briny sea taste of their juices. You could substitute mussels for the clams or shrimp for the lobster. Always ask your fishmonger about freshness and delivery days and buy what is freshest.

The first time I made this soup, I added fish sauce before tasting the broth and it was too salty, so make sure you taste it after the clams have opened and judge the saltiness for yourself.

Accompany this soup with a large green salad.

Serves 4

2 tablespoons canola oil

1 pound frozen lobster tails, shells reserved, meat
    sliced into ⅔-inch-thick pieces

2 large garlic cloves, minced

1 tablespoon chopped ginger

½ cup rice wine or sake

8 ounces rice noodles, soaked in a bowl of water for
    30 minutes

½ can coconut milk (7 ounces)

3 dozen littleneck or mahogany clams, scrubbed and soaked
    in water for an hour, open shells discarded

½ pound sea scallops

1 tablespoon fish sauce, or more to taste

Cilantro sprigs for garnish

1. Heat the oil in a large saucepan or chef's pan and add the lobster shells. Fry them until they are bright red and very fragrant, about 10 minutes. Add the garlic and ginger and continue to sauté while stirring for 2 minutes. Add 2 cups water and the rice wine and simmer gently for 10 minutes. Remove the lobster shells and set aside for garnish.

2. Bring a pot of water to a boil, drain the rice noodles, and cook them for 2 to 3 minutes. Drain and rinse with cold water.

3. Add the coconut milk to the broth while stirring. Once the broth begins to simmer, add the clams, cover the pan, and allow them to steam for 3 minutes. Lift the lid and add the scallops and lobster meat. Cover again and cook for an additional 2 minutes. Uncover and make sure that the clams are wide open and that the scallops and lobster meat are cooked through.

4. Taste for saltiness. If you need salt, add 1 tablespoon of the fish sauce, stir, and taste again. Add a second tablespoon if needed.

5. Put the noodles in the bottom of a large pasta bowl and pour in the steaming soup. Garnish with the cilantro sprigs and the bright red lobster shells and serve at once.

Noodles

S team is rising from a massive pot on the back of the stove. On my left, Rosa, the calm Peruvian, peels and deveins shrimp without looking. To my right, Achim, the stalwart Algerian we trained to become a first-class Asian chef, is creating a beautiful noise with wok and paddle. Emilio, the Mexican dishwasher with the irrepressible swagger, appears in the nick of time with an impossibly tall stack of bowls. I am somewhere in the middle with my head full of a dozen details. In a flash it all comes together in one bowl, which is placed before the customer who has been sitting at the counter watching it all: a vibrant sauce, barely cooked vegetables, dense slices of Chinese sausage, and a unifying blend of rice noodles. For a cook and restaurant owner, that look of pleasure on the customer's face is what it's all about. And there is something particularly appealing about a well-made noodle dish: it is a delightful meal in a bowl.

Since I exchanged my restaurant for a home and family, I see the bowl as just being bigger. Instead of preparing one noodle dish at a time, I now make one large batch and serve it on a single platter to four to six people, family style. While changing the scale can be tricky, I still get those gratifying looks of pleasure from family and friends.

Standard home kitchen stovetops don't generate enough heat to cook efficiently in a wok, especially when noodles are involved. The heat is distributed better if it has a flatter surface, so I use a chef's pan or a large sauté pan for stir-frying. Once the noodles have been added to a stir-fried dish, I put in the liquid and cover the dish. This works well, and you use less oil than you would in typical stir-frying.

Cold noodles tend to stick together once they are cooked, dried rice noodles in particular. Cook the noodles at the last minute, then dress and serve immediately. Egg noodles will hold up well for a day in the refrigerator if you toss them with chicken broth once they have been drained. Hearty soba noodles just need refreshing with cold water before serving. Cellophane noodles must be well combined with the dressing before serving to soak up the flavor.

Regarding noodles salads, tossing the noodles with the other ingredients before serving solves the sticking problem, but your presentation will suffer. To avoid this, I spoon a little of the dressing over the plain noodles on the platter and then more over the ingredients that top the noodles.

Most of the recipes in this chapter can be served alone as a complete meal. These were among the most popular dishes I served at my restaurant. They now get raves in my home kitchen.

Sesame Noodles

Who doesn't like sesame noodles? Unfortunately, the noodles served at Chinese restaurants are frequently pre-mixed and soggy with too much sesame paste and no fresh ginger. Here, the flavors are balanced, and refreshingly crunchy cucumber and cooked chicken soak up the rich sauce. Make an extra-large batch of sauce, and use what's left over as a dip for vegetables or fried tofu. I keep some on hand to spread over a chicken or grilled vegetable sandwich. To make this a vegetarian dish, omit the chicken and substitute vegetables and deep-fried tofu. I use any combination of julienned red bell pepper, carrot sticks, steamed green beans, and sliced cauliflower. Slice the deep-fried tofu into thin strips and toss with the vegetables before covering with sauce.

Chinese sesame paste is made from toasted sesame seeds; Middle Eastern tahini from raw white seeds. The Chinese version has a nuttier taste, but use tahini if that's all you can find.

Serves 4

½ cup Chinese sesame paste or tahini
    (the oil will have separated from the paste;
    stir to combine before measuring)
6 tablespoons soy sauce
2 tablespoons chopped ginger
4 garlic cloves, minced
4 teaspoons sugar
4 tablespoons sesame oil
4 drops chili oil, or more to taste
1 pound boneless, skinless chicken breasts
1 large cucumber

1 pound thin Chinese egg or wheat noodles, or thin
   spaghetti
1 teaspoon sesame seeds (optional)

1. Put the sesame paste, soy sauce, ginger, garlic, sugar, sesame oil, and chili oil in a small bowl. Use a fork to combine the sauce ingredients. Add ¼ cup water and keep stirring until you have a smooth sauce. Set the sauce aside.

2. Bring 3 cups water to a boil in a frying pan, put in the chicken, and lower the heat to a simmer, and cover. Poach until just cooked through, about 10 minutes. Remove the chicken with a slotted spoon. When it's cool, slice the chicken into ¼-inch pieces.

3. Peel the cucumber, cut it in half lengthwise, and remove the seeds with a spoon. Slice into ¼-inch-thick half-moons.

4. Bring a large pot of water to a boil and cook the noodles, loosening the bundles with tongs, until just done, 5 to 8 minutes. Drain and rinse in cold water.

5. Put the noodles in a large serving bowl and top with the sliced chicken and cucumber. Spoon half of the sauce over the noodles. Garnish with the sesame seeds, if using. Serve the rest of the sauce in a small bowl for people to add as desired.

Egg Noodles with
Indonesian Peanut Sauce and Apples

This is a chunky, uncooked peanut sauce traditionally served with satay. At the restaurant, I wanted something to serve over cold egg noodles that would contrast with our smooth sesame sauce and be substantial without meat. A surprising number of people don't know the difference between sesame sauce (made from ground sesame seeds) and peanut sauce (made from ground peanuts), so I wanted to make the difference abundantly clear. This combination of freshly roasted peanuts, coconut milk, herbs, and fresh lime juice does the trick, making for a rich, fulfilling, slightly exotic dish.

You can serve this as an appetizer, for lunch with a tossed salad, or as an accompaniment to Lemongrass Pork Chops (page 122) at dinner.

Serves 4

1 cup raw peanuts

2 large garlic cloves, chopped

1-inch piece ginger, coarsely chopped

½ bunch cilantro, chopped

2 teaspoons sambal olek

½ cup coconut milk

2 tablespoons fish sauce

1 tablespoon soy sauce

Juice of 1 lime

1 tablespoon sugar

¼ cup peanut or canola oil

1 pound thin Chinese egg or wheat noodles

1 tart apple, such as Granny Smith, cored and sliced
    at the last minute

1. Roast the peanuts in a 350°F oven or toaster oven until golden brown, 10 to 15 minutes. Remove and let cool.

2. In a food processor or blender, combine the garlic, ginger, and cilantro. Pulse until well blended. Add the peanuts and continue to pulse until the peanuts are well chopped—but don't let the sauce become a paste. Empty the contents into a small bowl and add the sambal olek, coconut milk, fish sauce, soy sauce, lime juice, and sugar, stirring in the oil last, a little at a time. Let the sauce sit at room temperature for an hour before serving to let the flavors meld. You can make and refrigerate the sauce up to a day in advance; just bring it back to room temperature before you assemble the dish.

3. Shortly before serving, bring a large pot of water to a boil and cook the egg noodles, loosening the bundles with tongs, until just done, 5 to 8 minutes. Drain and rinse them with cold water. Combine the noodles with the sauce in a large mixing bowl and toss well. Transfer the noodles to a serving bowl and fan the apple slices in a circle as garnish.

Asian Pesto

In this stylish twist on classic Italian pesto, I use peanuts instead of pine nuts, peanut oil instead of olive oil, and three herbs—cilantro, mint, and Thai basil—in place of Italian basil. I've made it with different herbs, depending on what I had on hand (once I even added marjoram to supplement a short supply of basil) and it is always good: fresh, rich, and aromatic. Thai basil gives this dish the right flavor, so make an extra effort to get some. If you can't find it, however, regular basil will do. Italian pesto uses Parmesan cheese to intensify its savoriness; this recipe uses only salt, so make sure you use enough or the flavor of the herbs will be lost.

Serve these noodles with Thai Beef Salad (page 118).

Serves 4

½ cup raw peanuts

2 garlic cloves, peeled

1 large bunch basil (2 cups tightly packed leaves, plus
     sprigs for garnish)

1 bunch mint (½ cup tightly packed leaves, plus sprigs
     for garnish)

1 bunch cilantro (1 cup tightly packed leaves, plus sprigs
     for garnish)

1 teaspoon salt, or more to taste

Juice of 1 lemon

½ cup peanut or canola oil

1 teaspoon chili sauce

1 pound thin Chinese egg or wheat noodles,
     or thin spaghetti

Lemon wedges

Herb sprigs

1. Roast the peanuts in a 350°F oven or toaster oven until golden brown, 10 to 15 minutes.

2. Grind the garlic in a food processor or blender until it is finely minced. Add the peanuts and process again until the peanuts are chopped into very small pieces—don't let them turn into a paste. Transfer the mixture to a large bowl.

3. Process the herbs in small batches until finely minced (reserve a few sprigs for garnish). Add them to the bowl. Stir in the 1 teaspoon salt, lemon juice, oil, and chili sauce. Make sure everything is well combined. Add a bit more oil if necessary. The pesto should be loose but not excessively oily. Let the pesto rest for 15 minutes, then taste to see if it needs more salt (I find that it usually needs a heaping teaspoon total).

4. Bring a large pot of water to a boil and cook the noodles, loosening the bundles with tongs, until just done, 5 to 8 minutes. Drain and rinse with cold water.

5. Add the noodles to the sauce in the bowl and toss thoroughly with tongs. Do this just before serving for the freshest taste. Transfer the noodles to a large serving bowl. Garnish with lemon wedges and a few sprigs of herbs.

Note: This sauce can be made in advance and stored in the refrigerator for several days. The color will change from bright to dull green but the flavor will hold.

Szechuan Chicken Salad

Chicken salad recipes are good things to have in your repertoire. They make for a nice lunch any time of the year, a light supper in the summer, or one of many dishes on a buffet. I hand-shred the chicken for a nicer texture. Noodles in cold salads have a tendency to clump and stick together. Instead of adding extra oil to keep them separate, I reserve some of the chicken poaching liquid to toss with them.

If you want to serve this salad for a main course, I would suggest a first course of Fried Oysters with Cilantro Sauce (page 46).

Serves 4

1 pound boneless, skinless chicken
    breasts
¾ pound green beans
3 celery stalks, sliced diagonally into ¼-inch-thick pieces
12 ounces thin Chinese egg or wheat noodles
2 large garlic cloves, minced
1 tablespoon minced ginger
3 scallions, thinly sliced
¼ cup unseasoned rice vinegar
1 tablespoon Chinese black vinegar, or
    balsamic vinegar
2 tablespoons sesame oil
6 tablespoons soy sauce
1 teaspoon coarsely ground black pepper
1 tablespoon sugar
4 drops chili oil, or more to taste
Cilantro sprigs for garnish

1. Bring 3 cups water to a boil in a frying pan, add the chicken, lower the heat to a simmer, cover, and poach until just cooked through, about 10 minutes. Remove the chicken with a slotted spoon and reserve the poaching liquid. When the chicken is cool enough to handle, tear the meat into thin strips by hand.

2. Blanch the green beans in boiling water until just done and still bright green. Rinse in cold water. Cut the beans into 2-inch pieces.

3. Put the chicken, beans, and celery in a bowl.

4. Bring a large pot of water to a boil and cook the noodles, loosening the bundles with tongs, until just done, 5 to 8 minutes. Drain and rinse with cold water. Shake the colander and let the noodles sit for 5 minutes. Add a cup of the reserved poaching liquid to the noodles in the colander and toss with tongs.

5. To make the dressing, combine the garlic, ginger, scallions, rice vinegar, black vinegar, sesame oil, soy sauce, black pepper, sugar, and chili oil in a small bowl and stir well to dissolve the sugar. This much can be done in advance. Refrigerate everything for up to 2 hours, but let it come back to room temperature before you assemble the salad.

6. When you are ready to serve, arrange the noodles on a serving platter. Add half of the dressing to the chicken, beans, and celery. Toss to coat. Spoon the remaining dressing over the noodles. Pour the chicken mixture onto the noodles and garnish with the cilantro sprigs.

Vietnamese Chicken Salad

In Vietnam, bits of grilled meat, chicken, and fish are always served with "table salad." This consists of lettuce leaves, chiles, herbs, rice papers or noodles, and nuoc cham, the national dipping sauce. The diner wraps the meat, chiles, vegetables, and herbs in rice paper or lettuce, then dips the wraps in the sauce. This dish combines everything into a salad with nuoc cham as the dressing. The result is a meal that pays homage to the hallmarks of Vietnamese cooking—its reliance on bright flavors and bountiful supplies of fresh herbs—and puts them in a user-friendly setting. I am leaving garlic out of the nuoc cham in this recipe as I did at the restaurant, to make it very clean and herbal.

If you are inclined, instead of the poached chicken breast, you could make Thai Grilled Chicken (page 110), slice it, and serve it in the salad.

This meal is perfect all by itself on a hot summer night.

Serves 4

DRESSING

1 tablespoon white distilled vinegar

⅓ cup fish sauce

3 tablespoons lime juice

2 tablespoons sugar

2 teaspoons chili sauce

½ cup raw peanuts

1 pound boneless, skinless chicken breasts

¼ pound mixed salad greens

2 carrots, grated

10 ounces rice noodles, soaked in a bowl of water for
   30 minutes

2 stalks broccoli, blanched and separated into florets
2 cups mixed cilantro, mint, and basil leaves
1 jalapeño chile, thinly sliced into rings

1. To make the dressing, combine the vinegar, fish sauce, lime juice, sugar, and chili sauce in a small bowl with 2 tablespoons water and stir to dissolve the sugar. Set the dressing aside at room temperature.

2. Roast the peanuts in an oven or toaster oven at 350°F until golden brown, 10 to 15 minutes. Cool and chop them coarsely by hand or in a food processor.

3. Bring 3 cups water to a boil in a frying pan, add the chicken, lower the heat to a simmer, cover, and poach until just cooked through, about 10 minutes. Remove the chicken with a slotted spoon; when cool, cut it into ½-inch-thick slices.

4. Bring a large pot of water to a boil. Line a platter with the salad greens and carrot. Spread the broccoli around the edge.

5. The noodles should be cooked at the last minute so they don't get sticky. Drain the soaked rice noodles, cook them in the boiling water for 2 minutes, drain again, and rinse with cold water. They should still be chewy.

6. Heap the noodles in the center of the platter and put a few spoonfuls of dressing on them. Top the noodles with the chicken and sprinkle the peanuts over the whole salad. Cover the top with all the herbs and spoon some more dressing over the entire salad. Serve the sliced chile on the side.

Thai Glass Noodle Salad

Called cellophane noodles, glass noodles, or bean threads, these unusual noodles are made from mung bean starch. They are most noted for the interesting, gelatinous texture they have when cooked and the way they soak up flavors. In Asia, ground pork is used in this salad, but I prefer ground turkey for a cold salad, which adds meatiness and is less fat.

Thai salads are comprised of a mix of elements, each adding a distinct flavor and texture. Although this type of salad is frequently served with crispy fried onions or chopped peanuts on top—feel free to try either—I find that those toppings weigh down the salad. Instead, I finish the salad with just the fresh herbs, chile, and onion.

Serve Lemongrass Soup (page 68) before this salad.

Serves 4

2 tablespoons canola oil

¾ pound ground turkey or chicken

½ pound medium shrimp, peeled and deveined

5 ounces cellophane noodles, soaked in water for
15 minutes and cut into 6-inch lengths with scissors

Juice of 2 limes

4 tablespoons fish sauce

1 tablespoon sugar

¼ red onion, chopped

¼ cup cilantro leaves

¼ cup mint leaves

1 jalapeño chile, thinly sliced into rings

3 cups red leaf lettuce, torn into small pieces

1. Heat the oil in a frying pan over medium heat and sauté the turkey until cooked through. Remove with a slotted spoon and drain on a paper towel.

2. Bring a small saucepan of water to a boil, reduce the heat to a simmer, and poach the shrimp until pink and curled, about 30 seconds. Drain and let them cool. Cut each shrimp in half lengthwise. Put the shrimp and turkey in a large bowl.

3. Bring a medium pot of water to a boil. Drain the noodles and cook them in the boiling water for 2 minutes. Drain them again and rinse with cold water. Try to shake as much water as possible from the colander.

4. To make the dressing, combine the lime juice, fish sauce, and sugar in a small bowl. Stir to dissolve the sugar. Add the noodles, onion, cilantro, mint, and jalapeño to the bowl. Pour the dressing over the top and mix everything thoroughly with tongs.

5. Arrange the lettuce on a platter or in a pasta bowl and heap the salad in the middle.

Singapore Noodles

Singapore noodles are commonly served at Chinese restaurants as a tangle of stir-fried noodles with curry powder and little else. My version is more complex, with shrimp, vegetables, Chinese sausage, and a sauce that is given depth with ginger, garlic, and scallions. It should be quite spicy, so add more dried chiles if that suits your taste.

Chinese pork sausage has a unique, sweet flavor, unlike any other sausage that I have tasted. One of my regular customers once described it as little packets of flavor that explode in your mouth. Chinese sausage is really essential to this recipe: if you can't get it, make something else. Substituting Italian sweet sausage or chorizo just doesn't work.

Serve the noodles alone or with a light first course like Roasted Asparagus with Miso Dressing (page 48).

Serves 4

4 tablespoons canola oil

1 tablespoon minced ginger

3 garlic cloves, minced

3 dried red chiles

3 scallions, thinly sliced

½ cup soy sauce

2 tablespoons Madras curry powder

1 pound medium shrimp, peeled and deveined, shells
    reserved

1 pound skinless chicken thighs

5 to 6 links Chinese sausage, thinly sliced on
    the diagonal

1 small head Savoy cabbage (1 pound), thinly sliced

3 large carrots, grated

12 ounces rice noodles, soaked in a bowl of water for
   30 minutes
1 cup bean sprouts (optional)

1. Heat a tablespoon of the oil in a small saucepan and sauté the ginger and garlic for a minute. Crumble the chiles into the pan and add one-third of the sliced scallions. Sauté while stirring for 2 minutes. Mix the soy sauce with the curry powder in a small bowl, stir to mix, and add to the pan. Bring the mixture to a boil and remove from the heat.

2. Add the reserved shrimp shells and chicken thighs to 4 cups water in a small saucepan and simmer until the chicken is cooked through, about 15 minutes. Strain the broth, reserving the chicken. Add a cup of this stock to the curry mixture and stir to mix, reserving the remainder of the stock. When the chicken is cool, pull the meat from the bone in small pieces and put it in a small bowl.

3. Stir-fry the sausage in a small, dry frying pan over medium heat for 5 minutes. Remove with a slotted spoon and drain on a paper towel. Add the sausage to the curry mixture. This much can be done in advance.

4. About 15 minutes before you want to serve, heat the remaining 3 tablespoons oil in a large sauté pan (with a lid) over medium-high heat. When it's hot, add the cabbage and carrots and stir-fry for 3 minutes. Add the raw shrimp and cooked chicken, stirring to combine. Drain the noodles, pour in the sauce, and top with the noodles. Pour a cup of the reserved shrimp-chicken broth over the whole thing. Cover and let cook for 5 to 8 minutes. Lift the lid several times to recombine with tongs. Make sure that the shrimp is cooked through and the noodles are chewy but cooked.

5. Place on a serving platter and top with the bean sprouts, if using, and the remaining scallions.

Noodles

Korean Beef Noodles

I'll never forget stepping out of the airplane in Seoul and smelling garlic in the air. If garlic is the national ingredient of Korea, chiles and sesame oil come in second and third. I wanted a dish that highlights all three elements and shows off the Korean flair for the rich and savory. Stir-frying the garlic with beef and meaty mushrooms and serving it over thick, chewy noodles results in a deeply satisfying all-in-one meal. It is very quick-cooking, so have everything ready to go at once.

Serve this with a green salad.

Serves 4

1⅓ pounds flank steak

3 tablespoons canola oil

½ pound portobello or shiitake mushroom caps, sliced

½ cup soy sauce

2 tablespoons sesame oil

2 tablespoons sugar

12 ounces Chinese wheat noodles or udon

4 large garlic cloves, minced

4 scallions, thinly sliced

1 dried red chile, broken in half

2 carrots, grated

1. Slice the flank steak diagonally against the grain into thin, 3-inch-long pieces. Set aside at room temperature.

2. Bring a large pot of water to a boil. Meanwhile, heat the oil over medium heat in a chef's or sauté pan and sauté the mushrooms until soft and juicy, about 5 minutes. Remove from the pan with a slotted spoon, leaving any oil and juice.

3. Combine the soy sauce, sesame oil, and sugar in a small bowl and stir to dissolve the sugar. Put the noodles into the boiling water. When the water comes back to a boil, turn the heat under the chef's pan to high; when hot, add the garlic, half of the scallions, and the chile. Stir-fry for a minute. Add the carrot, steak, and mushrooms. Stir-fry the meat for 2 to 3 minutes. Don't overcook it—it should be rare. Add the sauce and cook for 2 more minutes.

4. Cook the noodles until tender, 8 to 10 minutes, drain, and transfer to a serving bowl. Top with the beef mixture and garnish with the remaining scallions.

Yakisoba

Yakisoba is Japanese street food. In Tokyo, we lived on the edge of a park that hosted an annual plum blossom festival in March, and I have vivid memories of the groups of neighbors gathered beneath the white blossoms, and, there to feed them, the yakisoba man, decked out in his red-and-white bandanna before a huge griddle of these noodles, flipping with all his might. Served in that traditional way, yakisoba is an oily but tasty business plopped unassumingly onto a plate, with a blob of bright red pickled ginger on the side. It is made not with soba, as you might expect, but with the Chinese-style ramen noodle. My version is lighter and less oily, but very flavorful. A nice dish for a cool fall or winter day.

Use fresh noodles if you can get them—sometimes you can find fresh thin wheat noodles in the health food section of the grocery store. They cook faster than dried noodles.

At dinner, you could serve this after a first course of Roasted Asparagus with Miso Dressing (page 48).

Serves 4

1 pound pork loin or pork chop meat

⅓ cup soy sauce

⅓ cup rice wine

1½ tablespoons sugar

12 ounces Chinese wheat noodles or udon

3 tablespoons canola oil

1 onion, thinly sliced

1 pound napa or Savoy cabbage, thinly sliced

3 carrots, grated

1 tablespoon chopped ginger

2 scallions, thinly sliced

1. Cut the pork into thin 3-inch slices against the grain. Combine the soy sauce, rice wine, and sugar in a small bowl. Stir to dissolve the sugar.

2. Bring a large pot of water to a boil and cook the noodles until just done, about 8 minutes once the water has returned to a boil. Drain and rinse with cold water. The recipe can be made in advance to this point. The final assembly takes 10 to 15 minutes.

3. Heat the oil in a large sauté or chef's pan (with a lid) over medium-high heat. Add the onion and stir-fry for 3 minutes. Add the cabbage, carrot, and ginger. Stir-fry until the cabbage is wilted, 3 to 5 minutes. Add the pork and continue stir-frying for 2 minutes. Put the noodles on top of the mixture and pour the sauce over the whole thing.

4. Cover and cook for 3 to 5 minutes. Lift the lid and combine the mixture with tongs so that everything is well mixed. Make sure the pork is cooked but remains tender. Transfer to a serving platter and garnish with the scallions.

Southeast Asian Sauté with Shrimp, Spinach, and Coconut Milk

I created this dish as a very simple coconut milk stir-fry. It is elegant and hearty—and practically foolproof.

Coconut milk is to Southeast Asian food what cream is to French food. It magically transforms a dish. It adds richness, depth, and a silky, exotic flavor. In Asia, it is made from freshly grated coconut meat soaked in water. The liquid is strained and used for cooking. Fortunately, the canned coconut milk available to us is a good and convenient substitute. Buy a Thai brand if possible. Make sure to shake the can well before you use it.

The type of noodle used is crucial to the success of the dish. Use a thick wheat noodle to soak up the rich sauce—either Japanese udon or Chinese Shanghai or Canton noodle. Italian pasta should not be substituted, as semolina flour and coconut milk do not go well together.

At my restaurant I served this dish with chicken breast, pork, shrimp, or vegetables and spinach. At home, I've made it with shrimp or bay scallops and halved cherry tomatoes instead of spinach (cook the tomatoes a few minutes longer before adding the shrimp).

Serve this with a green salad.

Serves 4

12 ounces udon noodles

2 tablespoons canola oil

1 tablespoon chopped ginger

2 large garlic cloves, minced

6 ounces spinach, cleaned and torn into small pieces

3 tablespoons fish sauce

1 pound medium shrimp, peeled and deveined

½ can coconut milk (7 ounces) mixed with ½ cup water

1. Bring a large pot of water to a boil and cook the noodles until just done, about 8 minutes after the water has returned to a boil. Drain and rinse with cool water.

2. Heat the oil in a large sauté pan over medium-high heat. When it's hot, add the ginger and garlic. Stir-fry for a minute. Add the spinach and fish sauce and stir-fry for 2 minutes. Add the shrimp and stir-fry until just pink and curled, about a minute. Add the coconut milk mixture, stir once, and add the drained noodles. Use tongs to combine the mixture in the pan.

3. When heated through, 3 to 5 minutes, transfer the noodles to a large pasta serving bowl.

Pad Thai

Pad Thai is *the* best-known Thai restaurant dish. My version—a blend of rice noodles, shrimp, chicken, and lots of fresh vegetables, perfumed with Thai basil—is lighter, cleaner, and less sweet and oily than the typical rendition, but hearty and deeply satisfying. This recipe, which developed over time at the restaurant, owes as much to my customers and cooks as to my input. My kitchen was open, and customers would lean over the counter, peer over the cook's shoulder, and beg, "Less oil!" "*No* oil!" This is difficult to do for quick service in a wok, and my cooks complained bitterly, but what people wanted was a complete, healthy, flavor-packed meal in one bowl.

This makes a tasty but relatively tame dish. If everyone you are serving likes spice, use 2 tablespoons chili sauce in the recipe. Either way, have a bottle of sriracha chili sauce on the table.

You can easily make this dish for nonchicken eaters by omitting the chicken and using 1½ pounds of shrimp instead. Just boil the shrimp shells in 3 cups water for 10 minutes to make the stock.

My husband's all-time favorite is to have this with a first course of Spicy Chicken Wings (page 36).

Serves 4

½ cup raw peanuts

1 pound boneless, skinless chicken breasts

1 pound medium shrimp, peeled and deveined, shells reserved

⅓ cup fish sauce

Juice of 2 limes

1 tablespoon chili sauce

1 tablespoon shrimp powder

Everyday Asian

1½ tablespoons sugar

12 ounces rice noodles, soaked in a bowl of water for
     30 minutes

¼ cup canola oil

1 large onion, thinly sliced

3 carrots, grated

1 small bunch broccoli, separated into florets

½ cup Thai basil leaves, or Italian basil leaves

1 cup bean sprouts

1 lime, sliced into wedges

1. Roast the peanuts in a 350°F oven or toaster oven until golden brown, 10 to 15 minutes. Cool and chop coarsely.

2. Bring 3 cups water to a boil in a medium frying pan and put in the chicken, reduce the heat to a simmer, cover, and poach until just done, about 10 minutes. Remove the chicken with a slotted spoon, reserving the poaching liquid. When the meat is cool, slice it into ¼-inch-thick pieces and refrigerate.

3. Add the shrimp shells to the chicken poaching liquid and simmer for 5 minutes. Strain the broth.

4. Combine the fish sauce, lime juice, chili sauce, shrimp powder, and sugar in a medium bowl. Add 2 cups of the shrimp shell broth and stir to dissolve the sugar. This much can be done in advance.

5. About 15 minutes before you want to serve, heat the oil in a large sauté or chef's pan (with a lid) over high heat. Add the onion and stir-fry for a minute. Add the carrot and broccoli and stir-fry for 2 minutes. Add the shrimp, then the drained noodles, sauce, and chicken. Combine everything with tongs. Cover, reduce the heat to medium, and cook until the shrimp, noodles, and broccoli are just done. This will take 7 to 10 minutes. Lift the lid a few times to recombine with tongs. Add the basil for the last minute of cooking.

6. Heap the pad Thai on a large serving dish and top with the bean sprouts, crushed peanuts, and lime wedges.

Asian Barbecue

asians are great barbecuers because so much of their life is lived outdoors. Meals are often eaten on the street from carts and in casual restaurants. Small charcoal and wood-fired braziers are ubiquitous outside, even in colder countries like Japan and Korea. In South Asia the family kitchen is often outdoors, with charcoal as the main cooking fuel.

I love to grill anything, any time of the year (I've even grilled turkey on Thanksgiving). But the years I spent living in apartments taught me that for many people, a grill pan is a more realistic option. For some dishes, like grilled vegetables, they are actually preferable because small things won't fall into the fire. If you don't have a grill or grill pan, you can cook many of these dishes in the oven. The dish won't have a charcoal flavor, but the taste of the marinade will emerge more strongly.

As for cooking times, my estimates are for a fire that has just passed its peak and is on the way down. When you're grilling over charcoal, times will vary, depending on the amount of charcoal, distance from the grill to the charcoal, and how the charcoal is spread. Use your experience and your eyes to tell when the item is done. Different meats and fish can be served at different degrees of doneness according to your preference. For example, salmon fillet is fine slightly rare, while whole fish must be well cooked. Don't hesitate to cut into the meat or fish just to make sure it is done to your liking—that's better than taking it back to the grill.

There are different schools of thought about marinating. One school says that marinating meat is a waste of time and that only a dry rub should be put on the meat right before grilling and then a sauce added after. The other school claims that the longer you marinate the meat in a wet marinade the better; sauce is unnecessary. My recipes subscribe to both theories. I find a charcoal fire tends to suck a lot of the flavor out of a marinade, so make sure either that the marinade is deep in the meat or that you have a good sauce ready.

Indian Spice-Rubbed Pork Chops

This spice rub is so versatile that you can put it on pork chops, skewered prawns, chicken breasts, or even sliced eggplant. Dry rubs seal the juices into meat; these chops always turn out moist. I frequently make a larger batch of the rub and store it in a jar in my spice cabinet. Because this rub uses pre-ground spices, mixing them together in advance won't hurt the integrity of the spices. This dry rub also works well in a grill pan.

Serve this with jasmine rice and Lentils with Spinach (page 164).

Serves 4

Four ¾-inch-thick center-cut pork chops

1 tablespoon paprika

2 teaspoons turmeric

1 teaspoon salt

1 teaspoon freshly ground black pepper

½ teaspoon cayenne pepper

1. Mix the spices together in a small jar with a lid and shake them. Pour the rub on a large plate and shake the plate so that it is evenly coated. Lay the pork chops on the plate and then flip them over. Make sure they are evenly coated.

2. Let them sit at room temperature while you prepare your fire. Grill 5 to 7 minutes per side over glowing coals until crusty and yellow-orange.

Five-Spice Game Hens

Poultry, five-spice powder, and a grill are a classic combination, seen time and again in Chinese and Vietnamese cooking. Five is considered a healthy number, so much so that even if more than five spices are used in the mix, it's still referred to as five-spice. I find the aroma of this marinade very restorative and invigorating.

I use more five-spice than is typical, because I want it to be the dominant flavor. If you grind it yourself, it will not taste harsh. Chicken, poussin, or quail can be substituted for cornish game hens.

This entree is so versatile you can serve it with just about anything, but I like to pair it with homemade French fries for an Asia-meets-bistro touch.

Serves 4

2 Cornish game hens (3½ pounds total)

3 shallots or ½ onion, chopped

2 garlic cloves, minced

2 teaspoons five-spice powder

½ teaspoon black peppercorns, coarsely ground

3 tablespoons fish sauce

3 tablespoons soy sauce

3 tablespoons rice wine

2 tablespoons light brown sugar

1 tablespoon sesame oil

Cilantro sprigs for garnish

1. Cut the game hens in half down the breast bone and back-bone.

2. Combine the shallots, garlic, five-spice powder, and pepper. Mash it all together in a mortar or with the back of a fork in a small bowl. Add the fish sauce, soy sauce, rice wine, brown sugar, and sesame oil to the paste and stir to mix.

3. Put the hen halves in a shallow pan and rub the marinade into them with your hands. Cover the birds with cellophane and let them marinate in the refrigerator overnight or for at least 3 hours.

4. Prepare your grill and cook the game hens over hot coals until done, about 15 minutes per side. Serve on a platter garnished with the cilantro sprigs.

5. If you can't grill, bake the hens in the oven in a roasting pan with a rack at 350°F for 45 minutes, then turn the heat up to 400°F for a final 10 minutes.

Indonesian Grilled Chicken

Since grilled chicken can often be dry, a sauce is a welcome accompaniment. You could also prepare this dish satay style by skewering boneless chicken breast pieces, but chicken breasts on the bone have more flavor. Serve this with Green Bean Sambal (page 168) and jasmine rice, and Lemongrass Soup (page 68) for a nice first course.

Serves 4

1 large onion, coarsely chopped

1½-inch piece ginger or galangal, coarsely chopped

3 tablespoons soy sauce

½ teaspoon salt

2 tablespoons lemon juice

1 teaspoon sambal olek, or ½ jalapeño chile, coarsely chopped

2 tablespoons light brown sugar

1 tablespoon sesame oil

3 pounds chicken breasts on the bone (4 pieces)

2 tablespoons canola oil

½ cup coconut milk mixed with ½ cup water

Cilantro sprigs for garnish

1. Put the onion and ginger in a food processor and pulse until pureed. Add the soy sauce, salt, lemon juice, and sambal olek. Pulse again until well combined.

2. Empty the contents into a bowl and stir in the brown sugar and sesame oil until the sugar is dissolved. Add the chicken breasts and coat them thoroughly with the mixture. Allow them to marinate for 1 to 3 hours.

3. Prepare your grill. Remove the chicken from the marinade and grill until cooked through, 8 to 10 minutes per side, depending on how thick the breasts are.

4. While the chicken is grilling, heat the oil in a small saucepan over medium heat and fry the remaining marinade for a few minutes while stirring. Add the coconut milk mixture, reduce the heat to a simmer, and let the sauce cook for 5 minutes, stirring frequently.

5. Pour the sauce over the meat and garnish with the cilantro sprigs. You can line the platter with lettuce leaves, which taste great with the meat juice and sauce.

Thai Grilled Chicken

The marinade starts with the most basic of Thai seasonings: salt, peppercorns, and garlic, pounded in a mortar. In turn, shredded cilantro root (sometimes the roots are left on bunches of cilantro— buy them when you see them, chop them off, and freeze them), lemongrass, and lime juice are added. Rub it into the chicken flesh with your hands and allow to marinate overnight if possible. It is important to use skinless chicken pieces as the marinade doesn't penetrate the skin well.

Serve with jasmine rice and Thai Nam Prik with Crudités (page 60). You can put a little of the nam prik on the chicken.

Serves 4

2 garlic cloves, smashed with the side
  of a knife
2 teaspoons black peppercorns
2 teaspoons kosher salt
5 cilantro roots with 4 inches of stem, plus sprigs for
  garnish
2 lemongrass stalks, bottom 6 inches cut into 1-inch-thick
  pieces, bulbous ends removed
Juice of 1 lime
3 pounds skinless chicken thighs (about 8 pieces)

1. Pound the garlic, peppercorns, and salt together in a mortar or grind in a clean coffee grinder and put in a large bowl.

2. Grind up the cilantro roots in a food processor or blender with a couple of pulses and add them to the bowl.

3. Put the lemongrass in a clean coffee grinder or food processor and pulse a few times. The pieces should be nicely shredded. Add them to the mixture along with the lime juice.

4. Stir to mix and add the chicken pieces to the bowl. Rub the marinade in by hand. Cover and refrigerate overnight or for at least 3 hours.

5. Prepare your grill. Once the coals are glowing, cook the chicken 10 to 15 minutes per side until cooked through. Or roast the chicken in the oven in a pan with a rack at 400°F for 45 minutes. Serve on a platter garnished with the cilantro sprigs.

Pepper-Marinated Salmon

Whether cooked outdoors on the grill or indoors on a grill pan, this simple salmon recipe is perfect year-round. Nicely crisped skin is the secret to grilled salmon, so make sure your fire is not too hot or the skin will burn.

If using a grill pan, here's a tip for getting rid of that lingering fishy odor in the kitchen. While doing the dishes after dinner, bring a small saucepan of water to a boil, add a few star anise, a cinnamon stick, a spoonful of fennel seeds, and a few pieces of lemon rind. Let boil for 10 minutes; the smell will be gone.

Serve with jasmine rice and a soupy side dish such as Spiced Yellow Split Peas (page 162).

Serves 4

1½ pounds salmon fillet

1 teaspoon black peppercorns, coarsely ground

3 tablespoons fish sauce

2 scallions, chopped

Mint sprigs for garnish

1. If you are using a grill pan, cut the salmon into two or three pieces to fit in the pan neatly. If grilling outdoors, leave it whole.

2. Combine the peppercorns, fish sauce, and scallions in a pan large enough to hold the fish in a single layer. Stir to mix. Add the salmon and allow it to marinate for an hour at room temperature or 2 to 3 hours in the refrigerator. Turn the salmon two or three times as it marinates.

3. Prepare your fire and wait for glowing coals. Grill the fish skin side down, in a special fish basket if you have one, for about 8 minutes. You don't want the skin to be totally charred, but you do want it crispy. Flip carefully with 2 spatulas, or flip the basket. The other side should take only 5 minutes. Serve on a platter garnished with the fresh mint sprigs.

Grilled Striped Bass with Ginger Sauce

This classic Vietnamese ginger sauce is not for the meek. Intense with the fire of chiles, ginger, sugar, and lime, it gives an otherwise mild grilled fish a feisty new dimension.

Grilling whole fish can be a delicate operation. Brush the grill or grill basket with oil and make sure that the fish is done on the first side. If it is, the skin shouldn't stick. For best results, use a grilling basket, but I have also had good luck with two spatulas and a deep breath. A grill pan brought mixed reviews from my recipe testers. Make sure the grill pan is well oiled to prevent sticking.

Scallion garnishes are easy to make and look nice with fish. Cut the root ends off 4 scallions. Cut the other end to make each scallion 4 inches long. Cut several vertical slits 1½ inches from the end on both sides. Refrigerate the scallions in a bowl of cold water for an hour. The scallions will open up on the ends and make a pretty garnish.

Serve with a first course of Spicy Chicken Wings (page 36), followed by a tossed salad and jasmine rice.

Serves 2

Kosher salt

1 whole striped bass (1½ pounds when cleaned), washed and patted dry

GINGER SAUCE

2 tablespoons chopped ginger

1 large garlic clove, chopped

1 dried red chile

2 tablespoons sugar

½ lime

2 tablespoons fish sauce

Scallions for garnish

1. Generously salt the skin of the fish and set aside on a plate.

2. Make the sauce by combining the ginger, garlic, chile, and sugar in a mortar or small bowl and mash the ingredients together until they form a paste. Peel the lime but leave the membrane on. Mash this into the mixture. When it is well combined you can remove the membrane, as the pulp will be incorporated into the sauce. Stir in the fish sauce and 2 tablespoons of water.

3. Grill the fish 8 to 10 minutes per side or until well cooked. Transfer to a platter and garnish with the scallions. Serve the sauce on the side, preferably in two small bowls for dipping.

Grilled Squid Salad

Grilling squid transforms its flavor and makes its chewiness very appealing and savory. Unlike the deep-fried calamari served in Italian restaurants, this preparation is light and refreshing. It can be served as an appetizer, a light lunch, or accompaniment at dinner. Buy fresh squid with shiny, somewhat firm bodies; dull white, flaccid squid will be tough.

Shredding lemongrass pieces in a coffee grinder is a good idea—the lemongrass available to us here can be tough and difficult to chew if cut into the thin rings usually suggested in recipes.

Serves 4

1 lemongrass stalk, bottom 6 inches
    cut into 1-inch pieces, bulbous end removed
½ head Savoy cabbage, thinly sliced
½ sweet onion, thinly sliced
½ jalapeño chile, or more to taste, thinly sliced into rings
½ cup cilantro leaves, plus sprigs for garnish
2 tablespoons fish sauce
Juice of 1 lime
1 teaspoon sugar
1½ pounds cleaned squid, preferably with 5-inch-long bodies

1. Put the lemongrass pieces into a clean coffee grinder and pulse a few times. Remove the shredded lemongrass to a large bowl and add the cabbage, onion, chile, and cilantro. Toss to combine.

2. Combine the fish sauce, lime juice, and sugar in a small bowl. Stir to dissolve the sugar. Add this to the cabbage mixture and toss thoroughly.

3. Heat a grill pan over medium-high heat. Brush the pan generously with oil and put in as many squid as the pan will hold. They will start to shrivel up; do your best to keep them flattened out. Place the tentacle pieces in the pan along with the bodies. Turn after 2 minutes and cook the other side. When white throughout and springy to the touch, remove to a plate to cool. Cook all the squid this way. While they're still warm, slice the bodies into 1-inch rings.

4. Arrange the cabbage mixture on a platter and top with the warm squid rings, tentacles, and any juice that may have accumulated in the pan, which will further dress the salad. Garnish with cilantro.

5. Alternatively, grill the squid outdoors in a grill basket. Brush the squid with oil and enclose them in the basket. Grill for a few minutes per side.

Thai Beef Salad

This salad is searing, charcoally, zesty, and nearly foolproof. Its essence is the classic Thai marinade of cilantro roots, black pepper, garlic, and fish sauce. Thai salads, or *yums,* are intense affairs: no lettuce is involved and the "vegetables" are usually shallots, lemongrass, chiles, and herbs. My version retains the intensity of flavor but is more recognizable as a salad to Westerners. The meat can be served hot or at room temperature. If serving the salad cold, do not slice the meat until the last minute or it will turn gray. I have tried this recipe with skirt, flank, sirloin, and hanger steak as well as beef tenderloin. Flank steak is the winner because it cuts easily into even slices, has little fat and therefore can be cooked in a grill pan, and stands up well to a marinade.

It is important to use the cilantro roots when making this marinade. Sometimes they are left on the bunches: buy them when you see them, chop them off, and save them in the freezer. Cilantro should be soaked in a bowl of water before being spun dry because it holds a lot of dirt and grit as stubbornly as spinach does.

Serve with Asian Pesto (page 84) as a first course or as a first course before Singapore Chile Shrimp (page 138).

Serves 4

1 bunch cilantro with roots

2 garlic cloves, peeled

2 teaspoons black peppercorns, coarsely ground

¼ cup fish sauce

1 pound flank steak

SALAD DRESSING

¼ cup fish sauce

Juice of 2 limes

1 teaspoon chili sauce

1½ tablespoons sugar

1 small garlic clove, minced

6 cups mixed salad greens (mesclun mix or arugula, radiccio, and red leaf)

1 red onion, thinly sliced

1 jalapeño chile, thinly sliced into rings (optional)

1 bunch mint, leaves removed

Cilantro leaves

1. Clean the cilantro, reserving the roots. In a food processor, mortar, or blender, combine the roots, garlic, and pepper. Process until well chopped. In a pan large enough to hold the steak, combine the garlic mixture with the fish sauce and stir.

2. Add the steak to the pan and turn it over a few times to thoroughly coat with the mixture. Marinate the beef for at least an hour at room temperature or 3 to 6 hours refrigerated. Do not marinate overnight—it will become too strong.

3. To make the dressing, combine the fish sauce, lime juice, chili sauce, sugar, and garlic plus 2 tablespoons of water in a small bowl and stir to dissolve the sugar. Set the dressing aside.

4. Prepare the grill and cook the steak over hot coals until rare, about 7 minutes per side.

5. Spread the salad greens over a serving platter. Slice the steak on the diagonal into ¼-inch-thick pieces and lay it on top of the greens. Top with red onion, chile, and lots of mint and cilantro leaves. Spoon the dressing sparingly over the salad and serve the remaining dressing on the side.

Bulgogi

My visit to Seoul, Korea, was spent mostly waiting in line at the embassy for my Japanese work visa, but once out on the street I was tantalized by the alluring aroma of garlic and grilled meat. Everywhere I turned, irresistible cooking smells wafted out of open restaurant doors and from the charcoal braziers of street vendors. The omnipresent Korean ingredients of beef, garlic, sesame seeds, sesame oil, soy sauce, and scallions come together here in a classic preparation. A grill pan works very nicely for this dish. Serve these beef skewers with Sesame Spinach (page 161) and jasmine rice.

Serves 4

1 pound flank steak

3 tablespoons sesame seeds

2 tablespoons light brown sugar

1 tablespoon sesame oil

2 garlic cloves, minced

½ cup soy sauce

8 ounces mixed salad greens

2 scallions, thinly sliced into rings

1. Slice the flank steak against the grain into ¼-inch-thick slices and put them in a nonmetallic bowl.

2. Toast the sesame seeds in a dry frying pan over medium heat until they are light brown and fragrant, about 5 minutes, shaking the pan frequently. Cool the sesame seeds and grind them to a powder in a clean coffee grinder.

3. Combine the powder with the sugar, sesame oil, garlic, and soy sauce and stir to dissolve the sugar. Pour the marinade over the beef and let it stand for 30 minutes to an hour unrefrigerated or up to 3 hours in the refrigerator.

4. Prepare the grill. Thread the beef on metal skewers or bamboo skewers that have been soaked in water for about 20 minutes. Grill over hot coals until medium rare, 3 to 5 minutes per side.

5. Remove the beef from the skewers and serve on a platter of lettuce leaves garnished with the scallions.

Lemongrass Pork Chops

In Vietnam, small pieces of pork are marinated and then skewered and grilled. Once cooked, the meat is wrapped in a lettuce leaf with a few herbs and dipped in nuoc cham, a tangy dipping sauce. Here, this approach is applied to pork chops. By serving the chops with a tossed salad with a generous amount of mint and cilantro, then dressing the salad with the dressing for Vietnamese Chicken Salad on page 88, you'll end up with a combination of flavors that closely matches the traditional Vietnamese dish. Marinate the meat for at least three hours—or overnight if you can. I have made these chops many times in a stovetop grill pan as well as on the grill.

For a more elaborate meal, serve this with a first course of Vietnamese Cabbage, Chicken, and Mint Salad (page 54), and Sautéed Broccoli Rabe (page 159) and jasmine rice to accompany the pork.

Serves 4

2 garlic cloves, minced

2 tablespoons light brown sugar

1 teaspoon black peppercorns, coarsely ground

2 lemongrass stalks, bottom 6 inches sliced into
   very thin rings, bulbous ends removed

2 tablespoons fish sauce

1 teaspoon sesame oil

1 tablespoon rice wine

Four ¾-inch-thick center-cut pork chops

Cilantro sprigs for garnish

1. Combine the garlic, sugar, and pepper in a bowl and mash with a fork. Add the lemongrass, fish sauce, sesame oil, and rice wine. Stir to mix. Pour the marinade over the pork chops and coat each one well. Let them marinate for at least 3 hours.

2. Prepare your grill and cook the chops over hot coals or in a grill pan for 5 to 7 minutes per side. Serve garnished with the cilantro sprigs.

Vietnamese Spareribs

China, Singapore, Vietnam, and Korea each have distinctive ways of cooking spareribs—grilled, baked, braised, fried, or deep-fried. Vietnamese ribs are marinated in a tomato paste mixture that is first fried in oil to intensify the tomato flavor. Allow them to marinate overnight for a deeper flavor, and baste the ribs with the leftover marinade as they cook.

Asian ribs are generally not served with a barbecue sauce.

Before marinating, for easy turning and even cooking, slice three-quarters of the way down between each rib, leaving intact the backbone that holds the rack together. It is quick work to make the final separation with a sharp knife after they are cooked. Spareribs are frequently served as an appetizer in Asia, so, if you like, after separating the ribs, chop each one in half with a cleaver and serve them before a meal.

Serves 4

½ onion, minced

2 large garlic cloves, minced

1 teaspoon black pepper, coarsely ground

2 tablespoons sugar

3 tablespoons fish sauce

2 tablespoons canola oil

2 tablespoons tomato paste

3 pounds pork spareribs, ribs separated but still attached to the rack (see headnote)

Cilantro sprigs for garnish

1. Combine the onion, garlic, pepper, and sugar in a food processor or blender and pulse until you have a rough paste.

Remove the mixture to a pan large enough to hold the ribs, add the fish sauce, and stir.

2. Heat the oil in a small frying pan over medium heat. Add the tomato paste and fry while stirring until it becomes shiny, about 5 minutes. Cool slightly and stir it into the onion paste.

3. Spread the marinade over the ribs, making sure you get between the ribs and under the flaps. Let them marinate for 3 hour or overnight. Try to let at least 2 hours of the marinating time be at room temperature.

4. Prepare your grill and cook over gray coals, turning frequently and basting with leftover marinade until well done, 30 to 40 minutes. Serve on a platter garnished with the cilantro sprigs.

5. Alternatively, you can separate the ribs completely with a sharp knife and bake them in a 400°F oven for 45 minutes to an hour. Stir them up in the pan a bit after half an hour.

Grilled Eggplant with Minced Pork Sauce

Pork and eggplant are a classic Asian combination. I have experimented with many different methods of cooking the eggplant, and I like the flavor and presentation of this one best because the eggplant stays in attractive, savory rounds. Though this recipe calls for large globe eggplant, you can also use Japanese (minature globe variety) or Chinese (long, pale purple ones). If using the smaller ones, slice them in half lengthwise, brush them with oil, and grill them until they are cooked through. When buying eggplant, make sure it is firm and not bruised.

Serve this dish with a green salad and jasmine rice.

Serves 4

1 pound large eggplant

¼ cup canola oil

1 pound ground pork

2 large garlic cloves, coarsely chopped

1 tablespoon chopped ginger

3 scallions, coarsely chopped

1 tablespoon salted black beans, soaked in 1 cup of
    water for 5 minutes and drained

4 ounces fresh shiitake mushrooms, thinly sliced

3 tablespoons soy sauce

1 tablespoon hoisin sauce

2 teaspoons sugar

1 dried red chile

Cilantro sprigs for garnish

1. Slice the eggplant into ½-inch-thick rounds, leaving the skin on. Heat a grill pan over high heat or prepare an outdoor

grill. Put the oil in a small bowl and brush each eggplant slice on both sides with oil. Place them on the grill or in the grill pan. Watch them carefully and turn them when they are soft and begin to shrivel, 8 to 10 minutes in a grill pan. Turn and cook the other side in this way and remove to a plate. Cook all the slices.

2. Cook the pork in a medium frying pan over medium heat until it is no longer pink. Remove it with a slotted spoon to a paper towel. Leave the meat juices in the pan.

3. Combine the garlic, ginger, scallions, and black beans in the container of a food processor, or in a mortar, and pulse until everything is well chopped.

4. Put this mixture in the frying pan and cook over medium heat for a minute. Add the mushrooms and continue to cook while stirring until they are soft, 3 to 5 minutes. Add the pork, soy sauce, hoisin, sugar, and ½ cup water, and crumble the chile into the pan. Simmer for 5 minutes.

5. Arrange the eggplant circles on the bottom of a platter and top with the hot pork mixture. Garnish with the cilantro sprigs.

Main Courses

One of the things that gives me the greatest pleasure is to serve a meal to people who supposedly don't care for Asian food—"meat and potatoes" types who find the foods of the East too spicy or "foreign" or fussy. I set before them a plate of meaty braised lamb shanks, or an inviting roast chicken with Szechuan peppercorns, or a "red-cooked" beef stew, then watch as they learn that an Asian entree can be as substantial and comforting as anything they've ever eaten.

The entrees in this chapter represent my hearty, full-flavored style of cooking. They are the mainstays of my everyday home-kitchen repertoire. I've also served many of them at holiday family gatherings, sometimes accompanied by roasted potatoes, tomato and onion salads, Brussels sprouts, maybe with a crusty loaf of French bread on the side. I've tried to include dishes that incorporate many Asian cooking techniques.

Fried Snapper with Sweet-and-Sour Chili Sauce

A whole fried fish makes a great presentation and is the centerpiece for a memorable Asian meal. Buy only fresh fish. Find out which days are fish delivery days at your market and ask the fishmonger to hold what you want. The eyes must be clear and the flesh firm. Make sure the scales are removed when the fish is cleaned.

A frying pan big enough to hold the fish comfortably is a must. Cut off the head or tail to make the fish fit; fry the head or tail elsewhere in the pan and reassemble it on the serving plate.

The oil in the pan must be very hot. Fry the fish on the first side long enough that it releases easily from the pan on its own and is well cooked. Make sure it's nice and crispy because this will be the displayed side. It takes longer to fry a whole fish than you would think, especially on a home stovetop. Be patient and test the fish for doneness by cutting to the center on the nondisplayed side.

A tomatoey, spicy–sweet, vinegary sauce—a combination of flavors common in Thailand and Singapore—is best on this type of fish.

Accompany this fish with plenty of jasmine rice and steamed Chinese or regular broccoli.

Serves 2

1 whole red snapper or sea bass
    (1½ to 2 pounds)
Kosher salt
Canola oil for shallow-frying plus 2 tablespoons
2 garlic cloves, minced
2 teaspoons minced ginger
3 scallions, thinly sliced into rings
2 large shallots or ½ medium onion, minced

1 whole jalapeño chile, chopped
1 large tomato, chopped
2 tablespoons white distilled vinegar
½ teaspoon kosher salt
3 tablespoons light brown sugar
1 heaping tablespoon tomato paste
1 tablespoon fish sauce or soy sauce
Cilantro sprigs for garnish

1. Rinse the fish under cool running water and pat it dry with paper towels. Sprinkle it lightly with kosher salt inside and out and set aside on a platter.

2. Heat the 2 tablespoons oil in a small saucepan or frying pan over medium heat and fry the garlic, ginger, 2 of the scallions, shallots, and half of the chile until soft, about 5 minutes. Add the tomato and cook to a pulp, 3 to 5 minutes. Add the vinegar, salt, brown sugar, tomato paste, and fish sauce and simmer for 5 minutes, stirring in the tomato paste so that you have a smooth sauce. Taste it for spiciness; it should have a kick along with the sweetness. Add more chile if necessary. You can prepare the sauce an hour in advance and reheat it right before serving.

3. Fill a large frying pan with ½-inch oil. Heat the oil over medium-high heat for about 10 minutes, until it is very hot but not smoking. Slide the fish in carefully and let it cook for 7 to 10 minutes on the first side. Do not touch it for the first 7 minutes, then see if it loosens from the pan easily. If it is totally free, gently turn it, otherwise continue to cook. The skin should be intact. Cook the second side for another 7 to 10 minutes until thoroughly cooked and remove it from the pan with two spatulas.

4. Drain the fish briefly on a paper towel and transfer to a platter. Pour the warm sauce over the top. Sprinkle with the last scallion and generously garnish the platter around the fish with the cilantro sprigs.

5. After you have removed the flesh from the first side at the table, remove the backbone to make the flesh from the second side easily accessible.

Thai Chili Fish

This is a quick-cooking fish stew, hot-and-sour style. The combination of flaky fish fillets and tomato in a sweet-and-spicy vinegar sauce is delicious. I use cod, haddock, scrod, or turbot, but any white, firm-fleshed fish will do. Serve it over rice noodle triangles, rice sticks, or rice. Accompany with sautéed spinach or steamed green beans. If you want a complete meal in a bowl, add a quarter head savoy cabbage, thinly sliced, and 8 dried Chinese mushrooms (soaked in warm water for 30 minutes, drained, hard stems removed, and caps quartered) to the sauce with the tomatoes and cook for 10 minutes before adding the fish.

Serves 4

1½ pounds cod fillets (or other firm,
    white-fleshed fish fillets)
3 tablespoons fish sauce
3 tablespoons white distilled vinegar
1 tablespoon sriracha chili sauce
1 tablespoon light brown sugar
3 tablespoons canola oil
1 large onion, thinly sliced
2 large tomatoes or 6 plum tomatoes, chopped
Cilantro sprigs for garnish

1. Cut the fish fillets into 2-inch-wide pieces. Combine the fish sauce, vinegar, chili sauce, and brown sugar in a small bowl. Stir to dissolve the sugar.

2. Heat the oil in a sauté pan over medium heat and add the onion. Cook while stirring until the onion is quite soft and light brown, about 15 minutes. Add the tomatoes and cook to a pulp, 5 to 10 minutes more. Add the fish sauce mixture and simmer for 2 minutes.

3. Add the fish pieces, stir, and cook until the fish is just done, 3 to 5 minutes. Garnish with the cilantro sprigs and serve at once.

4. The sauce can be made in advance. Just bring it back to a simmer and add the fish 5 minutes before serving.

Salmon with Tomato and Garam Masala

In Indian cooking, garam masala, a spice mixture of cardamom, peppercorns, cinnamon, cumin, and cloves, is added in the last few minutes of cooking or sprinkled over a finished dish, almost like a condiment. I prefer to add it with the other ingredients to soften the flavor. I recommend grinding the garam masala yourself. My young daughters, who won't touch onions or anything green, have to be held back from the serving dish. I once made this recipe with two pounds of salmon to assure that my husband and I would get a good-sized portion.

Serve with rice and a green salad.

Serves 4

1½ pounds salmon fillet

3 tablespoons canola oil

1 large onion, chopped

¼ cup chopped cilantro leaves, plus sprigs for garnish

2 large garlic cloves, minced

1½ teaspoons cumin seeds, ground

1 teaspoon turmeric

¼ teaspoon cayenne pepper

2 large tomatoes or 6 plum tomatoes, chopped

2 teaspoons garam masala (see page 12)

1¼ teaspoons salt

2 tablespoons lemon juice

1. Slice the salmon fillet into 2-inch-wide strips.

2. Heat the oil in a medium sauté pan over low heat. Add the onion, cilantro, and garlic. Cook the mixture slowly, stirring occasionally, until the onion is golden brown, about 20 minutes. Add the cumin, turmeric, and cayenne pepper and cook for a minute. Add the tomatoes, garam masala, and salt. Cook the tomato to a pulp, 5 to 10 minutes. Add the lemon juice and stir to mix. The recipe can be made to this point up to 2 hours ahead of time.

3. Shortly before serving, reheat the sauce and add the salmon to the pan. Spoon the sauce over it. Cover and cook over medium heat, turning the pieces once, until the salmon is cooked through, 5 to 10 minutes. Garnish with sprigs of cilantro.

Chinese Fish Fillets with Black Beans

Whitefish fillets with black beans is a classic Cantonese dish. I add shiitake mushrooms to enhance the flavor. I always welcome a nice preparation for flounder or other mild whitefish; however, delicate whitefish fillets are very difficult to handle and tend to fall apart while cooking. To combat this, I let the fish firm up in egg white and a bit of cornstarch in the refrigerator for a few hours before cooking.

Serve this with a crisp green salad or sautéed greens and jasmine rice.

Serves 4

1 egg white

1 tablespoon plus 2 tablespoon rice wine

2 teaspoons cornstarch

½ teaspoon salt

1½ pounds flounder, sole, or tilapia fillets

3 tablespoons canola oil

2 large garlic cloves, minced

2 teaspoons minced ginger

2 scallions, thinly sliced into rings

1 tablespoon salted black beans, soaked in water for
     5 minutes, drained, and chopped

4 large shiitake mushrooms, stems removed,
     caps sliced into ½-inch-thick pieces

2 tablespoons soy sauce

Cilantro sprigs for garnish

1. Combine the egg white, the 1 tablespoon rice wine, cornstarch, and salt in a medium bowl and stir to mix. Dip each fillet into the mixture and place it in a shallow glass or ceramic

dish. When all of the fillets have been prepared, pour any remaining egg mixture over the top. Cover the pan and refrigerate for at least 2 hours.

2. Shortly before you are ready to serve, heat the oil in a medium frying pan over medium heat and add the garlic, ginger, scallions, and black beans. Stir-fry for 2 minutes. Add the mushrooms and cook for 2 more minutes. Add the soy sauce, the 2 tablespoons rice wine, and ¼ cup water.

3. When the sauce begins to simmer, add the fish fillets in one layer on top of the mushrooms. Cover the pan and reduce the heat to low. Check the fish in 3 to 4 minutes and gently flip the fillets. Cover again and cook until the fish is flaky, about 3 minutes.

4. Transfer the fish to a serving platter and pour the sauce over the fish. Garnish with the cilantro sprigs.

Singapore Chile Shrimp

The first time I went to Singapore, it was while traveling on the cheap from Indonesia to Thailand. Our money-saving method involved riding a ferry from Jakarta to a tiny Indonesian island off the coast of Singapore that had seemingly been developed solely to exploit travelers. We were required to spend the night in what was considered a "classy" hotel, eat in their restaurant, and then continue the next day by hydrofoil to Singapore. There were no local villages—just these strange cinder block hotels. That evening, as we complained about being stuck in this surreal place, we sat down to a fabulous dinner of chile prawns. It was an unforgettable meal: dining outdoors in the tropical night, looking across the bay at the lights of Singapore, and eating these delicious prawns.

If you can get prawns, use them; I call for shrimp as they are easier to find. I serve the shrimp with the shells on because the shells impart flavor, but my husband complains about the peeling. The recipe works just fine with peeled shrimp—it's up to you.

Serve this with a green salad and jasmine rice.

Serves 4

1½ pounds large shrimp (31–40 count),
   peeled and deveined
1 small onion, roughly chopped
½ red bell pepper, roughly chopped
1 large garlic clove, chopped
1-inch piece ginger, roughly chopped
½ teaspoon shrimp paste
1 tablespoon sambal olek
Two 2-inch pieces lemon zest, roughly chopped
3 tablespoons canola oil
1½ tablespoons light brown sugar

2 tablespoons fish sauce

1 dried red chile, broken into 3 pieces

1 teaspoon paprika

Juice of ½ lemon

½ teaspoon salt

Cilantro sprigs for garnish

1. Put the shrimp in a bowl of lightly salted water and refrigerate until you are ready to cook them.

2. Combine the onion, bell pepper, garlic, ginger, shrimp paste, sambal olek, and lemon zest in the container of a food processor or blender and process until a rough paste forms.

3. Heat the oil in a medium frying pan over medium heat. Add the spice paste and cook while stirring until it is a brownish orange color and the oil has separated, about 15 minutes. Add the brown sugar, fish sauce, chile, paprika, and ½ cup water. Stir to combine and dissolve the sugar. Cover the pan, reduce the heat, and simmer the mixture for 5 minutes. Uncover, add the lemon juice and salt, and stir to mix.

4. Increase the heat to medium-high, add the shrimp, and cook until they are just done, 3 to 5 minutes. Transfer to a serving dish and garnish with the cilantro sprigs.

Garlic Fried Shrimp

These shrimp are so savory and delicious, I bet you can't eat just one. The garlic is first caramelized with sugar, then the shrimp is fried in the same flavorful oil and finally combined with the garlic syrup. It is a Vietnamese method usually seen with hard-shell crabs. It is best if you leave the shells on the shrimp; I think they add a lot to the dish and it is fun to suck the shells to get every bit of flavor. For easy eating, buy large shrimp.

Serve this with jasmine rice and Arugula Salad with Deep-Fried Tofu (page 59).

Serves 4

1½ pounds large or extra-large shrimp
6 tablespoons canola oil
4 large garlic cloves, minced
½ onion, thinly sliced
2 tablespoons sugar
2 tablespoons fish sauce
½ teaspoon salt
½ teaspoon freshly ground black pepper
Cilantro sprigs for garnish

1. Devein the shrimp while leaving the shells on. To do this, lay them on a table and hold them in place with one hand while you slice through the shell down the back of the shrimp with a sharp knife from the top to the tail, about ¼ inch deep. Remove any black vein. Put the shrimp in a bowl of lightly salted water until you are ready to use them.

2. Heat the oil in a small saucepan over medium-high heat. Add the garlic and stir-fry for a minute. Add the onion and reduce the heat to low. Let the onion cook until it is very soft and transparent, about 15 minutes. Add the sugar and stir until it dissolves. Add the fish sauce, salt, and pepper and stir to combine, simmer for a minute, and remove from the heat. The mixture should look smooth and syrupy and the oil will have separated from the sauce.

3. Carefully pour the separated oil into a medium frying pan and heat over medium-high heat. Add the shrimp and stir-fry until they are cooked through and the shells are pink, 3 to 5 minutes. Add the sauce from the first pan, stir to combine it with the shrimp, and heat through. Transfer to a serving platter and garnish with the cilantro sprigs.

Burmese Chicken Coconut Curry

A Burmese-American woman named Mimi Khin worked at my restaurant for a few years; she generously shared with me her family recipes—of which this is one—and helped me simplify them for quick service. The food of Burma is touched by that of its bordering countries: India, China, and Thailand. This makes for a unique and extremely flavorful cuisine, where ginger, garlic, and turmeric (the three most dominant seasonings) are combined variously with soy sauce, coconut milk, Indian spices, dried shrimp in all its forms, and fish sauce. Garnishes are tremendously important in Burmese cuisine, adding many more layers of flavor. The national dish—mohinga, a fish soup—uses at least eleven garnishes. So please encourage your guests to squeeze the lime and eat the cilantro leaves and scallions.

This dish goes well with Sautéed Broccoli Rabe (page 159). To make it a bit more formal, serve Burmese Fish Cake Salad (page 52) as a first course.

Serves 4

3 tablespoons canola oil

1 large onion, thinly sliced

1 tablespoon chopped ginger

2 large garlic cloves, minced

1 teaspoon turmeric

2 teaspoons paprika

¼ teaspoon cayenne pepper, or more to taste

½ can coconut milk (7 ounces)

3 tablespoons fish sauce

1 cup chicken stock

12 ounces Chinese Canton noodles or udon

1½ pounds boneless, skinless chicken breasts, cut into
   ¼-inch-thick slices
1 lime, sliced into wedges
2 scallions, thinly sliced into rings
¼ cup cilantro leaves

1. Heat the oil in a large sauté or chef's pan. Cook the onion, ginger, and garlic over low heat until golden brown, 20 to 30 minutes. It is very important not to rush this.

2. Turn the heat up to medium. Add the turmeric, paprika, and cayenne. Stir well and cook for a minute. Add the coconut milk, fish sauce, and chicken stock. Stir to mix and continue to cook for 5 minutes. Remove from the heat. This much can be done in advance.

3. Shortly before serving, bring a large pot of water to a boil. Meanwhile, reheat the sauce over medium heat, add the raw chicken slices, and cook until cooked through, 5 to 7 minutes. Add the noodles to the boiling water and cook until just done, 8 to 10 minutes. Drain the noodles and rinse with cool water.

4. Divide the noodles among four bowls and ladle the chicken curry over the top. Garnish with a sprinkling of scallions, lime wedges, and the cilantro leaves. You can also serve this from the table in a large pasta bowl.

Roast Chicken with Szechuan Peppercorns

Nothing beats a good roast chicken, and this recipe plays up its savory, comfort-food appeal by adding the unique flavor of Szechuan peppercorns. Szechuan peppercorns are not actually a member of the peppercorn family at all but are pods of the prickly ash. They are tremendously aromatic when roasted and add an exotic mouth-tingling quality to a dish. They are used to season meat as in this Chinese seasoning salt. It is often added after the meat is cooked but I like it as a spice rub.

When buying a whole chicken for Asian cooking, always try to find one that is between 3 and 3½ pounds. I think this is the best way to approximate the smaller fresh chickens you would find in Asia. Our chickens are frequently 4 to 5 pounds, and the ratio of white meat to skin and fat is far too high, which makes for dry chicken meat.

I recommend using the same spice rub on four 8-ounce beef tenderloin steaks and grilling them rare. It makes for a wonderful variation on steak au poivre.

Serve the chicken with simple roasted potatoes and Sautéed Broccoli Rabe (page 159).

Serves 4

2 teaspoons Szechuan peppercorns
1 teaspoon black peppercorns
2 teaspoons kosher salt
One 3½-pound whole chicken
Cilantro sprigs for garnish

1. Remove the backbone from the chicken by cutting down either side of it. Wash the chicken and pat it dry. Spread it out flat, breast side up.

2. Toast the Szechuan peppercorns in a dry skillet over medium heat until just smoking, 3 to 5 minutes. Cool and combine them with the black peppercorns in a mortar or clean coffee grinder. Grind to a powder. Combine the pepper mixture with the salt in a small bowl and rub it well into the chicken on both sides. Let it sit at room temperature for an hour.

3. Preheat the oven to 375°F and roast the chicken on a rack, breast up, for an hour. Garnish with the cilantro sprigs.

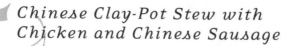

Chinese Clay-Pot Stew with Chicken and Chinese Sausage

This dish is a variant of an ancient Chinese cooking technique. Traditionally, it would be cooked in an clay pot. The pot is made of clay and sand and adds a deep, earthy flavor to a dish. If you have one, by all means use it, but this relatively quick-cooking recipe works well on top of the stove in a chef's or sauté pan with a lid. A whole cut-up chicken is generally used, but here I use boneless, skinless chicken breasts because the fatty sausage coats the chicken nicely, and you don't need the extra fat from the skin or dark meat pieces. Just make sure you don't overcook the white meat.

This dish really shows off the taste of Chinese sausage. It is a vital ingredient—there is no substitute. If you can get a package, make this recipe and the Singapore Noodles on page 92). Each recipe calls for half a package, and I guarantee that you will want to buy more.

Serve this hearty dish on a cold winter night with a big green salad.

Serves 4

1 pound boneless, skinless chicken
    breasts
2 tablespoons rice wine
1 tablespoon cornstarch
1 teaspoon salt
1 tablespoon sesame oil
2 tablespoons canola oil
½ head Savoy cabbage (1 pound), cored and cut into chunks
2 medium tomatoes, horizontally sliced
1 jalapeño chile, thinly sliced into rings

8 dried Chinese mushrooms, soaked in warm water for
   30 minutes, hard stems removed, caps cut in half,
   soaking liquid reserved
4 to 5 links Chinese sausage, sliced diagonally into thin
   pieces
2 tablespoons mushroom soy or regular soy sauce
Cilantro sprigs for garnish

1. Cut the chicken breasts into 2-inch pieces. Put in a bowl with the rice wine, cornstarch, salt, and sesame oil. Mix together with your hands. Set aside.

2. Heat the canola oil in a medium chef's pan or sauté pan over medium heat and add the cabbage. Stir-fry until the cabbage is somewhat wilted, about 3 minutes. Reduce the heat to low. Scatter the tomatoes, chile, and mushrooms on top of the cabbage mixture. Place the chicken pieces over the mushrooms, and finally the sausage on top.

3. Combine ½ cup of the mushroom soaking liquid with the soy sauce and stir to mix. Pour this mixture over the sausage and cover the pan.

4. Cook slowly until the chicken is cooked through, about 30 minutes once it begins to simmer.

5. Transfer the stew to a serving dish and garnish with the cilantro sprigs.

Thai Beefsteak Curry

Beef curries are eaten all over Southeast Asia. Bathed in coconut milk with a complex spice paste as a base, they are rich and delicious. In this quick-cooking Thai curry you use steak, and with good quality beef cooked rare, it is quite a treat.

You can use top sirloin steak for this dish—it is an economical cut and the sauce will tenderize it somewhat. As a grilling alternative, use skirt steak, which should be grilled rare, sliced, and then added to the curry for the last few minutes of cooking. This treatment works well for steak that has a bit of fat in it—the fat is grilled off and the dish doesn't become too greasy. Or, if you want an elegant meal, use beef tenderloin.

Serve this with jasmine rice and Green Bean Sambal (page 168).

Serves 4

3 tablespoons canola oil

1 onion, thinly sliced

1 cup coconut milk

2 tablespoons red curry paste

1 large tomato, coarsely chopped

1 pound top sirloin, grilled skirt steak, or beef tenderloin, sliced against the grain into thin 2-inch slices

8 ounces green beans, blanched in boiling water for 5 minutes, drained, and cut into 2-inch pieces

2 tablespoons fish sauce

2 kaffir lime leaves, or two 3-inch pieces of lime zest

20 Thai or Italian basil leaves, plus a sprig for garnish

1. Heat the oil in a medium sauté pan over medium heat. When it's hot, add the onion and sauté until it is light brown and very soft, about 10 minutes. Add ½ cup of the coconut milk. When it begins to bubble, add the curry paste and stir-fry for 2 minutes. Add the tomato and cook it to a pulp, about 5 minutes.

2. Add the steak and stir-fry in the spice paste until the steak is cooked rare, 3 to 4 minutes. Add the remaining ½ cup coconut milk mixed with ¼ cup water, the beans, fish sauce, and lime leaves.

3. Bring to a simmer, add the basil leaves, and stir. Serve immediately, garnished with a basil sprig.

Chinese Red-Cooked Beef Stew

"Red cooked" simply means slowly braised in dark soy sauce and other ingredients, a method that turns meat or chicken red in color with intense flavors. For tender but not dry stew, use two-inch cubes of beef chuck, not beef round, with plenty of marbled fat running through it. Meat that is floured and seared tends to become pasty and messy. To seal in juices, I prefer to boil the meat and then brown it without first flouring. Serve the beef stew over jasmine rice or on top of warm Chinese egg noodles with Tossed Salad with Lemon-Ginger Dressing (page 62) on the side.

Serves 4

2 pounds beef chuck, cut into
    2-inch cubes
4 tablespoons canola oil
1 onion, thinly sliced
3 garlic cloves, peeled and smashed
Three ¼-inch slices unpeeled ginger
½ cup soy sauce (if you have light and dark soy,
    use a half and half combination)
¼ cup rice wine
1 tablespoon light brown sugar
4 whole star anise
2-inch cinnamon stick
4 carrots, cut into 1-inch chunks
1 jalapeño chile, thinly sliced into rings
1 tablespoon cornstarch (optional)

1. Put the stew meat into a saucepan, just cover with water, and bring to a boil. Cook for 2 minutes and then drain the meat in a colander.

2. In a medium saucepan or chef's pan with a lid, heat the oil over high heat. Put in the beef cubes and quickly brown on all sides. Remove the meat from the pan, lower the heat to medium, and add the onion, garlic, and ginger. Cook until the onion is soft, 5 to 7 minutes. Add the soy sauce, rice wine, sugar, star anise, cinnamon stick, and beef cubes along with any accumulated juices. Add hot water to cover the meat; when it starts to boil, cover the pan and reduce the heat to very low. Let the stew simmer for a total of 2 hours. Check the pot periodically to make sure it is simmering gently.

3. Add the carrot pieces 20 minutes before the 2 hours are up.

4. Spoon off the grease floating on top of the stew before serving. You can either take the whole spices out of the dish, or warn your guests of their presence. Garnish with the chile slices, or serve them on a small plate on the side.

5. This stew doesn't have a thick gravy. If you want it thick, in the last 5 minutes of cooking, remove ¼ cup liquid from the pan and stir in the cornstarch until it is dissolved. Add this mixture to the stew, stir well, and continue cooking for 5 minutes.

Filipino Adobo with Pork and Chicken

The Philippines was ruled by Spain for more than three hundred years, and the cuisine reflects that. You find dishes cooked with olive oil, olives, tomatoes, and vinegar, right along with fish sauce and coconut milk. Adobo, which means cooked in a pickling style, is probably the best-known Filipino dish. It was originally conceived as a way of preserving meat before refrigeration. However, this dish, like Indian vindaloo (pork cooked with vinegar and spices), has remained popular because it adds a complexity of flavor to the meat. I like to cook this a day in advance and serve it cold for a picnic.

This dish is traditionally served with a plate of sliced tomatoes or a Filipino tomato salsa. I have served it with Carrot and Mustard Seed Salad (page 63).

Serves 4

1½ pounds country-style pork ribs
   on the bone
2 pounds skinless chicken thighs
¾ cup white distilled vinegar
4 large garlic cloves, peeled and smashed
½ small onion, sliced
3 tablespoons soy sauce
½ teaspoon salt
2 bay leaves
1 teaspoon black peppercorns, coarsely ground
6 tablespoons canola oil
Spinach leaves, washed and patted dry, to cover a platter

1. Combine the pork, chicken, vinegar, garlic, onion, soy sauce, salt, bay leaves, and black pepper in a chef's pan or medium saucepan and then add enough water just to cover the meat, 1 to 2 cups. Let the meat marinate for an hour.

2. Put the pan on a burner and bring it to a boil. Cover, reduce the heat to low, and simmer until the meat is quite tender, about 45 minutes.

3. Remove the meat from the pan, bring the liquid back to a boil, and reduce it to 1 cup. Strain the sauce and skim off the fat.

4. Heat the oil in a large frying pan over medium-high heat. Quickly fry the pork and chicken, turning once. You want a nice brown crust.

5. Reheat the sauce. Arrange the spinach on a serving platter and cover with the meat. Pour half of the sauce over the top and serve the rest on the side.

Mapo Tofu

Although it's a staple on Chinese takeout menus, I find it odd that mapo tofu is rarely well executed. If made as originally intended—with black beans, sesame oil, and lots of garlic to flavor the tofu and mushrooms—it is earthy and delicious. It's also a good dish to serve people who don't think they like tofu. Tofu, sold in sealed 15-ounce tubs, takes well to marinades and sauces. Before using, tofu must be well drained. Wrap it in paper towels and put a heavy plate on top for thirty minutes or so, pouring off liquid as it accumulates.

If you have an Asian market nearby or even a well-stocked supermarket, use the fresh cakes you'll find there floating in tubs of water. If you aren't going to use them that day, put them in a bowl of fresh water and change it daily, and they will last a few days in the refrigerator. You will find that they need much less draining time than the packaged variety.

This dish needs a vegetable side along with the rice. I would suggest a tossed salad or Sesame Spinach (page 161).

Serves 4

3 tablespoons soy sauce

3 tablespoons hoisin sauce

2 teaspoons sriracha chili sauce

1 teaspoon sugar

½ pound ground beef or pork

3 tablespoons canola oil

1 tablespoon salted black beans, soaked in a cup of water
    for 5 minutes, drained, and chopped

2 large garlic cloves, minced

3 scallions, thinly sliced into rings

8 dried Chinese mushrooms, soaked in a bowl of warm
    water for 30 minutes, drained, hard stems removed and
    caps sliced (½ cup soaking liquid reserved)
1 pound firm tofu, drained and cut into 1-inch cubes
1 tablespoon cornstarch
1 tablespoon sesame oil

1. Combine the soy sauce, hoisin, chili sauce, and sugar in a small bowl. Stir to dissolve the sugar.

2. Sauté the ground beef in a a medium frying pan over medium heat until no longer pink; remove with a slotted spoon, and drain on a paper towel. Pour the fat from the pan and add the oil.

3. Heat the oil over medium-high heat, add the black beans and garlic, and sauté for a minute while stirring. Add the ground beef, half the scallions, the mushrooms, tofu, sauce, and the reserved mushroom soaking liquid mixed with the cornstarch; stir until the cornstarch is dissolved.

4. Cook while stirring until the sauce is thick and the tofu is heated through, 5 to 10 minutes. Add the sesame oil for the last 2 minutes of cooking and stir to combine. Serve over rice, garnished with the rest of the scallions.

5. You can make this dish vegetarian by omitting the meat, in which case I would suggest using a combination of fresh and dried mushrooms. Try 10 dried mushrooms and 4 ounces of fresh shiitake mushrooms.

Chinese Roast Pork Tenderloin

Roast pork loin and whole roast duck hang in the windows of many Chinese restaurants. This prominent placement allows no mistaking their importance in the cuisine. They are used to add depth and flavor to many Chinese dishes. Roast pork can be found in fried rice dishes, soups, stir-fries, and braised dishes. This recipe is a variation of *cha siu,* traditional Cantonese roast pork; try making it at home if you don't live near a Chinese deli.

I recommend using pork butt or boneless country-style ribs for this dish. The extra fat in the meat melts and gives it a better flavor. When thinly sliced and piled on a crusty roll with sliced onions, this pork is great for sandwiches, but you could easily serve it sliced with grilled vegetables and pour some of the pork sauce over them, too. This sauce also works well on grilled pork or chicken.

Serves 4

1½ pounds small pork tenderloins,
    or 2 pounds pork butt or boneless country-style ribs
⅓ cup hoisin sauce
⅓ cup rice wine
⅓ cup soy sauce
1 tablespoon ketchup
2 large garlic cloves, minced
2 tablespoons light brown sugar
Cilantro sprigs for garnish

1. If using pork butt, cut it into 2-inch cubes and trim off the visible fat. If using ribs, separate them by cutting between each rib with a sharp knife. Otherwise, leave the tenderloins whole.

2. Combine the hoisin, rice wine, soy sauce, garlic, and brown sugar in a small bowl. Stir well and pour over the meat. Allow to marinate for 1 to 3 hours.

3. Preheat the oven to 400°F. Bring the marinade to a boil over high heat, lower the heat, and reduce slightly. Bake the tenderloin for 20 minutes, remove from the oven, and baste with the sauce. Put it back in the oven for 10 to 20 minutes, depending on how thick the tenderloin is, until cooked through. It should have a deep brownish red color and have little burned edges. The pork butt or ribs will take 40 to 45 minutes.

4. Heat the remainder of the sauce in a small saucepan over medium heat and allow it to simmer for 3 minutes. Remove the meat from the oven and let it rest for 5 minutes. Slice into ¼-inch-thick pieces. Serve garnished with the cilantro sprigs, with the sauce on the side.

Vegetables and Side Dishes

*t*he great variety of Asian vegetables is wondrous but can also be a source of frustration, since it's difficult for home cooks here to find bitter melon, luffa squash, fuzzy melon, water spinach, mustard cabbage, Chinese celery, flowering chives, long beans, green papaya, lotus root, or fresh bamboo shoots. In this chapter, I focus on recipes that use readily available vegetables, prepared in different ways.

I love Indian-style vegetables and legumes. Here I offer okra in a spice paste of onion, ginger, and garlic, layered with coriander, cumin, and turmeric. Cauliflower is cooked with whole spices that have been sautéed in hot oil with garlic. Green beans, potatoes, carrots, or cabbage can be used interchangeably in these preparations.

Sautéed greens and vegetables curries and sambals (chile-fried condiments) should also be part of your Asian vegetable repertoire and are just as versatile. Most any vegetable that is fresh at the market can be used.

Sautéed Broccoli Rabe with Caramelized Onions

This side dish goes well with most any main course or barbecued dish in this book. Everyone likes it, and broccoli rabe can be made an hour or two in advance and reheated at the last minute.

I have made this dish with many Asian greens as well as kale, collards, and spinach, but I like broccoli rabe the best. It holds its shape better than spinach and has a slightly bitter flavor. It makes a unique marriage of an Italian ingredient with Asian flavorings.

Cooking time will vary with the green. Spinach will cook the most quickly. Whatever the green, the key is not to overcook it. Stop the cooking when it is just tender and you can't go wrong.

Serves 4

1½ pounds broccoli rabe, Chinese
    broccoli, or spinach
1 onion, thinly sliced
2 tablespoons canola oil
1 tablespoon fish sauce, or more to taste

1. Chop the greens into 2-inch pieces, discarding the bottom 2 inches of stem, and soak them in a bowl of cold water.

2. Heat the oil in a large frying pan and cook the onion over medium-low heat until very brown and caramelized, 20 to 25 minutes.

3. Drain the greens and add them to the pan. Cook until the broccoli rabe is well wilted, 7 to 10 minutes. Add the tablespoon of fish sauce, stir, and taste for saltiness. Add a bit more if necessary and cook for a few more minutes.

Vegetable Curry with Coconut Milk

When making this Thai curry, I look for a nice mix of colors and textures. Whole white mushrooms work well, but for color I use tomatoes and snow peas for crunch. Try other combinations such as green beans, eggplant, and red bell pepper, or cabbage, cherry tomatoes, and okra.

Serves 4

3 tablespoons canola oil

1 onion, sliced

1 cup coconut milk

1 tablespoon red curry paste

1 large garlic clove, minced

10 ounces white button mushrooms

6 plum tomatoes, chopped into large pieces

2 tablespoons fish sauce

½ pound snow peas, strings removed

20 Thai basil or Italian basil leaves, plus a sprig for garnish

1. Heat the oil in a medium frying pan over medium heat until hot. Add the onion and sauté until golden brown, about 15 minutes. Add ½ cup of the coconut milk and when it begins to bubble, add the curry paste and stir-fry for a minute. Add the garlic and fry for another minute.

2. Add the mushrooms, tomatoes, the remaining ½ cup coconut milk mixed with ½ cup water, and the fish sauce. Stir to mix, cover the pan and reduce the heat to low. Simmer for 5 minutes. Add the snow peas and stir to combine. Cover again and cook until the peas are just done, about 5 minutes. Toss in the basil leaves and cook for a minute more. Transfer to a serving bowl, garnish with the basil sprig, and serve at once.

Sesame Spinach

The sharp, fresh greenness of this cold side dish makes a nice accompaniment to grilled meat or fish. A lot of spinach is required because it dramatically reduces in volume when cooked. Spinach is frequently served this way in Korea and Japan. The Japanese have a special device for grinding sesame seeds called a suribachi. It is a wonderful, inexpensive tool if you can get your hands on one, but, if not, a clean coffee grinder will do just fine. Serve with Bulgogi (page 120) or grilled pork chops and mashed potatoes.

Serves 4

1½ pounds spinach, stems removed, soaked in a bowl of water and drained but not dried

3 tablespoons sesame seeds

4 tablespoons soy sauce

2 teaspoons sugar

1 tablespoon unseasoned rice vinegar

2 tablespoons dashi (see page 11) or chicken stock

1. Put the spinach in a large, dry frying pan over medium heat. Cover and cook until the spinach is completely wilted, about 5 minutes. Drain in a colander and squeeze out any excess moisture. Chop the spinach coarsely.

2. Put the sesame seeds in a small, dry frying pan and toast over medium heat until light brown and fragrant, shaking the pan frequently, 3 to 5 minutes. Cool and grind the seeds to a powder in a clean coffee grinder.

3. Combine the soy sauce, sugar, rice vinegar, and dashi and stir until the sugar is dissolved. Add the sesame powder and stir until well blended. Arrange the spinach in four mounds on a small serving dish and pour dressing over each one.

Spiced Yellow Split Peas

These split peas, called chana dal, are a classic Indian legume—smaller and more savory than regular split peas. If you can't find chana dal, any yellow split peas will work nicely. A traditional Indian cooking technique is used here: simmering the split peas with turmeric and ginger slices until done, then frying whole spices in oil and tossing them in with the peas at the very end of the cooking process, infusing the peas with a rich complexity of flavors. I frequently eat this alone with rice for a simple, filling lunch. Making this dish in advance or even the day before only improves the flavor.

Serves 6

1½ cups yellow split peas or chana dal

½ teaspoon turmeric

Two ¼-inch-thick slices unpeeled ginger

1½ teaspoons salt

3 tablespoons canola oil

1 teaspoon cumin seeds

1½ teaspoons black mustard seeds

2 large garlic cloves, minced

1 dried red chile

1. Wash the split peas in a colander and pick over to remove anything that isn't a split pea. Bring 5 cups of water and the peas to a boil in a medium saucepan and skim off any scum. Add the turmeric and ginger slices. Stir to mix and turn the heat to low. Cover, leaving the lid slightly ajar. Let them simmer for 35 to 45 minutes, until tender. Remove the ginger slices and add the salt.

2. Heat the oil in a small frying pan over medium-high heat and add the cumin and mustard seeds. When the mustard seeds pop, add the garlic and break the chile up in the pan. Fry until the garlic is lightly brown, 1 to 2 minutes, and immediately pour the spices and oil into the split peas. Stir to mix, and cover. Turn the heat off and let the flavors combine for 5 minutes. Serve with rice.

Lentils with Spinach

When you want a side dish that adds heartiness to a meal but won't compete with the flavors of the entree, my favorite lentil dish is the ticket. It doesn't have garlic or onions, so there is a clean simplicity to it. This dish is very good reheated. Make it an hour or two before it is needed, turn off the heat, and let it sit on the burner, covered.

Serve alongside a steak, with salmon, or as part of a vegetarian meal.

Serves 6

1 cup lentils

12 ounces spinach

1 small bunch cilantro

3 tablespoons canola oil

1 tablespoon chopped ginger

½ jalapeño chile, or more to taste, chopped

1½ teaspoons salt

Juice of 1 lemon

1. Wash and drain the lentils. Add them to 3 cups water in a medium saucepan and bring to a boil. Cover the pan and reduce the heat to low. Simmer until tender but not mushy, 20 minutes. Remove from the heat.

2. Remove the stems from the spinach and cilantro and soak the leaves in a bowl of water. Drain the greens in a colander and taste them to make sure they are grit free (if not, soak them again). Chop the spinach and cilantro coarsely.

3. Heat the oil in a chef's pan over medium heat and add the ginger and chile. Cook for a minute, and then add the spinach and cilantro. Cover and reduce the heat to low. Check the pan after 5 minutes to see if the greens are wilted. If not, continue to cook while stirring until they are.

4. Add the salt and the lentils and stir to mix. Let them simmer on low for 10 minutes. Add the lemon juice and stir again. Simmer for a further 2 minutes. Transfer to a serving bowl.

Green Beans with Minced Pork

Using bits of meat as a flavoring for vegetables is a mainstay of Asian cooking. This dish is made throughout Asia with long beans, which are much longer, coarser, and more flavorful than our standard green beans. Use them if you can find them. In Chinese restaurants the beans are frequently deep-fried, but I cut the beans in smallish pieces, stir-fry them with the other ingredients, add a bit of stock, and let them simmer until done. They are less greasy that way and soak up the other flavors.

Serve with Chinese Fish Fillets with Black Beans (page 136) and jasmine rice.

Serves 4

½ pound ground pork

3 tablespoons canola oil

2 large garlic cloves, minced

2 dried red chiles, or more to taste

3 tablespoons fish sauce

1 tablespoon light brown sugar

½ cup chicken stock or water

1½ pounds green beans, trimmed and cut into
    1-inch pieces

1. Sauté the ground pork in a medium frying pan over medium heat until it is cooked through, remove with a slotted spoon, and then drain it on a paper towel. Pour off any pork fat but don't wipe out the pan.

2. Add the oil to the pan and sauté the garlic over medium heat. After a minute, break the chiles over the pan into two or three pieces and add them to the garlic. Continue to fry for

Everyday
Asian

another minute and then add the fish sauce, brown sugar, chicken stock, and beans and stir to combine. Bring to a simmer, then cover and lower the heat.

3. Let cook until the beans are done, 5 to 8 minutes. Transfer to a serving dish.

Green Bean Sambal

To build an Indonesian or Malaysian meal, start with a bowl of plain rice and a sambal, or chile-fried condiment. To this add a meat or fish curry, a soup, a vegetable dish, and krupah (friend shrimp crackers). The sambal should be intensely flavored so that a little goes a long way.

This sambal is chile-fried green beans, but cauliflower, chunks of fish, squid, or just chiles could be substituted. Small amounts of dried shrimp paste add just the right flavor to Southeast Asian dishes. It has an even stronger smell when being cooked (I happen to love the smell, but my daughter always says, "What stinks?"), but it soon vanishes, so don't be put off, just open a window.

This dish can be eaten warm or at room temperature. Serve it with lots of jasmine rice and Thai Beefsteak Curry (page 148).

Serves 4

2 tablespoons canola oil

1 small onion, finely chopped

2 garlic cloves, minced

2 teaspoons sambal olek

½ teaspoon dried shrimp paste

¾ pound green beans, ends removed and sliced into
   very thin pieces on the diagonal

¾ teaspoon salt

1. Heat the oil in a medium frying pan over medium heat. When it's hot, add the onion and garlic. Lower the heat and gently cook until golden brown, about 15 minutes.

2. Increase the heat slightly and add the sambal olek. Fry for a minute. Add the shrimp paste, crush it into the mixture with the back of a spoon, and cook for another minute. Add the green beans, salt, and ½ cup water.

3. Cover the pan, lower the heat, and simmer until the beans are cooked, 8 to 10 minutes. Lift the lid for the last 2 minutes and allow some of the liquid to boil off to intensify the flavor.

4. Transfer to a small serving bowl.

Okra with Tomato Chile Paste

Okra is a swing vegetable—just as prominent along the Ganges as it is in the Mississippi Delta. Indians love it because it holds its shape well, has an unusual appearance, and an interesting texture and flavor. I like it best in a tomato-flavored sauce with a bit of lemon juice. Fresh okra should have few if any black spots, and when you bend the tip it should snap off easily. If nibbled raw, it should be crisp, not woody.

I served this dish one Christmas Eve to a vegetarian gathering with Lentils with Spinach (page 164), an eggplant dish, and Carrot and Mustard Seed Salad (page 63). It was a big hit.

Serves 4

1 medium onion, roughly chopped

2 garlic cloves, roughly chopped

1-inch piece ginger, peeled and roughly chopped

3 tablespoons canola oil

1 teaspoon cumin seeds, ground

1 teaspoon coriander seeds, ground

½ teaspoon turmeric

1 dried red chile, broken into 3 pieces

2 small tomatoes, chopped

1 pound okra, both ends cut off and sliced into
    1-inch lengths

1 teaspoon salt

2 tablespoons lemon juice

1. Put the onion, garlic, and ginger in a food processor and process until a paste forms. Add a tablespoon or two of water if needed.

2. Heat the oil in a medium frying pan over medium heat and cook the paste until it is light brown, 5 to 7 minutes. Add the cumin, coriander, turmeric, and chile. Cook while stirring for 2 minutes. Add the tomatoes and cook to a pulp, about 5 minutes. Add the okra, salt, and ¼ cup water.

3. Cover and cook the okra until it is just soft, about 10 minutes. Add the lemon juice and cook for an additional minute.

Eggplant Puree

Every cuisine has its version of eggplant puree. In the Middle East it is babaganoush. The French make an eggplant caviar. Indians serve pureed eggplant mixed with yogurt. Thais offer an eggplant nam prik, or dipping sauce. This version of the Thai nam prik is thicker and I serve it as a condiment to accompany grilled meat. Do not puree the eggplant too much; the texture should be slightly chunky.

Serves 4

1 medium eggplant

Two ¼-inch-thick slices red onion or 1 large shallot,
    roughly chopped

1 garlic clove, roughly chopped

½ serrano chile, or more to taste, roughly chopped

1 teaspoon sugar

1 tablespoon shrimp powder (optional)

2 tablespoons fish sauce

Juice of 1 lime

20 mint leaves, rolled up and julienned

1. Preheat the oven to 375°F. Pierce the eggplant in several places with a fork. Roast the eggplant on the bare oven rack until quite soft, 30 to 40 minutes. (Put a pan underneath to catch any juice.) Remove the eggplant from the oven and cool.

2. In a food processor or blender, pulse the onion, garlic, and chile until finely chopped. Remove the skin from the eggplant, chop the eggplant coarsely, and add it to the food processor. Pulse a few times so that it is well broken up but not fluffy.

3. Transfer the eggplant to a mixing bowl and add the sugar, shrimp powder, fish sauce, lime juice, and mint. Stir to mix. Cover and refrigerate for at least an hour before serving.

Spiced Cauliflower

Indian culinary and cultural influences can be found throughout Southeast Asia. Malaysia and Singapore have large Indian populations, and Burmese cuisine has strong Indian elements because its border is shared with India and Bangladesh. I was much taken with the Indian banana leaf restaurants in Singapore. You receive a silver tray lined with a banana leaf. Waiters come around and deliver dollops of vegetarian specialties, such as this spiced cauliflower, along with a dal, basmati rice, a yogurt dish, and a chutney.

Serve with Indian Spice–Rubbed Pork Chops (page 105) or Roast Chicken with Szechuan Peppercorns (page 144) and rice.

Serves 4

1 head cauliflower, separated into florets

4 tablespoons canola oil

1 tablespoon black mustard seeds

2 garlic cloves, minced

1 teaspoon fennel seeds

½ teaspoon turmeric

1 dried red chile, torn into pieces

1 teaspoon salt

1. Soak the cauliflower in a bowl of cold water for 20 minutes. Drain.

2. Heat the oil in a medium frying pan over medium-high heat. Add the mustard seeds. When they pop, add the garlic and fennel seeds. Stir the spices while cooking for 2 minutes. Add the turmeric and chile. Stir again. Add the cauliflower and stir while cooking for 2 to 3 minutes. Add ½ cup water and the salt, cover, and reduce the heat to low. Simmer until the cauliflower is cooked through but not mushy, 10 to 15 minutes.

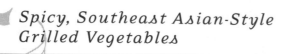

Spicy, Southeast Asian-Style Grilled Vegetables

A grill pan makes grilling vegetables so easy that you can feel free to experiment with anything that looks good at the market, but a combination of complementary vegetables such as eggplant slices, sweet potato slices, asparagus, cauliflower, zucchini, and scallions works very well. Grilled red potato slices make a refreshing alternative to roasted or baked potatoes.

Serve these grilled vegetables with any roasted or grilled meat or chicken.

¼ cup canola oil

Serves 4

1 large sweet potato, peeled and sliced
 into ¼-inch-thick diagonal slices
4 small zucchini, ends removed and sliced in half
 horizontally
8 cauliflower florets

DIPPING SAUCE
2 tablespoons fish sauce
Juice of 1 lime
1 tablespoon sugar
½ serrano chile, thinly sliced into rings

Heat a grill pan over medium-high heat. Put the oil in a small bowl. Brush each vegetable piece with oil and place it in the grill pan. Watch things carefully. Turn when cooked on one side, and cook the other side the same way. Different vegetables take different amounts of time to cook. Cauliflower needs a long time because of its shape. This amount of vegetables should take 30 to 40 minutes all together. Meanwhile, make the dipping sauce by combining all the ingredients in a small bowl and stirring to dissolve the sugar. Arrange the vegetables on a platter and either pour the sauce over the top or serve it on the side.

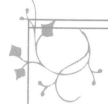

DESSERT

The best way to finish an Asian meal is with a platter of sliced tropical fruits. Simultaneously sweet and thirst-quenching, they are just the thing to cut through the heat and humidity of Southeast Asia. The fruits of the region—mangosteens, rambutans, starfruit, jackfruit, durian, watermelon, pineapple, papaya, pear apples, coconut, mangoes, and on and on—are so exquisite in their natural settings that they alone are almost worth the trip. Since many of these fruits are not readily available in the West, use fresh, seasonal fruit, local whenever possible. Slices of watermelon, cantaloupe, papaya, mango, or pineapple make a nice accompaniment to an Asian meal. During the winter, when fresh fruit is limited, serve Granny Smith apples and banana slices or juicy orange wedges. I serve a lime wedge with a platter of sliced fruit as they do in Asia. A squirt over the top turns a plate of fruit into a fruit salad.

If you have to have something else, try the Sesame Butter Cookies. The recipe was given to me by my mother many years ago.

SESAME BUTTER COOKIES   MAKES 2 DOZEN 2-INCH COOKIES

2 sticks butter

⅔ cup sugar

2 cups all-purpose flour

1 teaspoon vanilla

½ cup sesame seeds

Cream the butter with the sugar in a bowl. Add the flour, vanilla, and sesame seeds and stir until a rough dough forms. Roll the dough into balls and place on an ungreased cookie sheet. Press the balls flat with a floured glass bottom. Bake in a 375° oven for 10 to 12 minutes.

Fruit sorbet is also a good option for an Asian dessert. However, my favorite dessert with most any Asian meal is green tea ice cream—made with Japanese green tea in powdered form. Unfortunately, while it's a standby at Japanese restaurants, it's rarely available at the retail level. Depending on where you live, you may periodically find Asian ice creams like red bean, green tea, mango, and ginger at Asian grocers or by telephoning boutique ice cream producers.

WHAT TO DRINK WITH ASIAN FOOD

There can be no doubt, tea is *the* drink served before, after, or during meals at home throughout Asia. Japan and China have many varieties appropriate with meals: green, black, oolong, and jasmine, to name a few. Tea drinking in those countries has been elevated to a high art with the tea ceremony in Japan and the lavish tea houses of Hong Kong.

Other Asian countries may drink their tea in more humble circumstances, but they are devoted to it nonetheless. In Indonesia, Malaysia, and Singapore where there are large Muslim populations and alcohol is forbidden, sweet teas are consumed with the same enthusiasm as in the Middle East. In Burma, additives to the tea actually stain the teeth yellow (how appropriate for a country where turmeric is rarely left out of a dish). And in Vietnam, after the long French colonial period when coffee drinking was the fashion, they have returned to tea. The exception to the tea rule is the Philippines, where they drink hot chocolate (perhaps because of their long association with Spain) and soft drinks with meals.

Thais drink very strong, very sweet, milky tea and coffee. They add sweetened condensed milk to strong coffee or tea and serve it hot or over ice.

Ginger iced tea is an authentic and refreshing companion to Asian foods. Pour boiling water into a cup with three quarter-inch slices of ginger and allow to steep for 15 minutes. Sweeten with honey or sugar to taste, then pour over ice.

Fresh fruit juices and coconut water (the liquid inside a coconut) are also common, although these drinks are taken more as refreshing snacks than as a beverage to accompany meals. Nonalcoholic, cool, and refreshing, lemonade or limeade go well with these meals. If you have a juicer, I recommend trying either fresh watermelon, pineapple, or green apple juice.

If alcohol is served, it will more than likely be beer, which is widely produced in Asia. In the hot and humid weather, beer cuts the spiciness of the food without clashing with the flavors. To my mind, Asian beer is the perfect match for an Asian meal: even the look of the bottle on the table adds to the atmosphere. I like to match the beer with the cuisine: if you are cooking adobo, get Philippine San Miguel; with Japanese salt-grilled fish, serve Kirin; Singha goes perfectly with a Thai curry; and on a hot day a cold Tsingtao is the ideal match for Szechuan chicken salad.

Matching Asian foods with wine is a bit tricky because of the strong spices and flavors. Here are some guidelines to follow.

- For dishes with a coconut milk base (Southeast Asian Sauté, Burmese Chicken Coconut Curry), a creamy California-style Chardonnay is a good accompaniment.

- Meat dishes with a soy sauce influence (Japanese Yakisoba, Korean Beef Noodles, Red-Cooked Beef Stew), pair well with a fruity Zinfandel or a smooth Merlot.

- If the dish is highly spiced with chiles or chili sauce (Singapore Noodles), a Riesling or Gewürztraminer works well. The spiciness of the wine blends nicely with the spiciness of the food.

- The wine that stands up the best to the majority of the dishes in this book is Sauvignon Blanc. Its high acidity makes it a very good food wine in general. The strong flavors used in some of the dishes—fish sauce, vinegars, and citrus juice—are generally considered hard to match with wine, but in many cases Sauvignon Blanc, with its herbal and mineral flavors, makes a fresh match.

Source Guide

Thai Grocer
1430 N. Bosworth Ave., 1st floor
Chicago, Il 60622
773-988-8424
Fax 773-871-3969
www.thaigrocer.com

Asia Foods
18-20 Oxford St.
Boston, MA 02111
877-902-0841
Fax 617-426-3252
www.asiafoods.com

Temple of Thai
P. O. Box 112
Carroll, IA 51401
877-811-8773
fax 712-792-0698
www.templeofthai.com

Ethnic Grocer
162 W. Hubbard St., 3rd floor
Chicago, Il 60610
312-527-2800
Fax 312-723-9471
ethnicgrocer.com
(click on country)

Spice Merchant
P. O. Box 594
Jackson Hole, WY 83001
800-551-5999
fax 888-538-9305 (toll free)
www.emall.com (click on food
and then click on oriental cooking secrets)
(It is best to call this source and
get the catalog)

Index

bass, grilled striped, with ginger
   sauce, 114–15
beans, *see* black beans; green
   beans
beef:
   in bulgogi, 120–21
   ground, in mapo tofu, 154–
      55
   Korean beef noodles, 94–95
   -steak curry, Thai, 148–49
   stew, Chinese red-cooked,
      150–51
   Thai beef salad, 118–19
   Vietnamese beef pho, 66–67
beverages, 178–79
black beans:
   salted, Chinese fish fillets with,
      136–37
   salted, in grilled eggplant with
      minced pork sauce,
      126–27
   salted, in mapo tofu, 154–
      55
bok choy, in Chinese cellophane
   noodle and pork soup,
   72–73
broccoli:
   in pad Thai, 100–102
   in Vietnamese chicken salad,
      88–89
broccoli rabe:
   sautéed with caramelized
      onions, 159
   in Singapore mah mee with
      shrimp, roast pork, and
      egg noodles, 74–75
bulgogi, 120–21
Burmese:
   chicken coconut curry, 142–
      43
   fish cake salad, 52–53

*C*abbage, napa:
   in Chinese cellophane noodle
      and pork soup, 72–73
   in yakisoba, 96–97
cabbage, Savoy:
   chicken, and mint salad,
      Vietnamese, 54–55
   in Chinese clay-pot stew with
      chicken and Chinese
      sausage, 146–47
   in grilled squid salad, 116–17
   in Indonesian gado gado, 50–51
   in Singapore noodles, 92–93
   in yakisoba, 96–97
carrot(s):
   in Chinese red-cooked beef
      stew, 150–51
   in Indonesian gado gado, 50–51
   in Korean beef noodles, 94–95
   and mustard seed salad, 63
   in pad Thai, 100–102
   in Singapore noodles, 92–93
   in Thai nam prik with crudités,
      60–61
   in Vietnamese cabbage, chicken
      and mint salad, 54–55
   in Vietnamese chicken salad,
      88–89
   in yakisoba, 96–97
cauliflower, spiced, 173
cellophane noodles, 18
   and pork soup, Chinese, 72–73
   in Thai glass noodle salad,
      90–91
   see also noodles
chana dal, *see* split peas, yellow
   spiced
chicken:
   Chinese clay-pot stew with
      Chinese sausage and,
      146–47

Index

8/15 (33) 3/14
9/08 16 1/08
9/04 10 6/04